COACHING
COMBINATION PLAY

FROM BUILD UP TO FINISH

WRITTEN BY

TAG LAMCHE

PUBLISHED BY

COACHING
COMBINATION PLAY

FROM BUILD UP TO FINISH

First Published July 2016 by SoccerTutor.com
Info@soccertutor.com | www.SoccerTutor.com
UK: 0208 1234 007 | **US:** (305) 767 4443 | **ROTW:** +44 208 1234 007
ISBN: 978-1-910491-11-9

Copyright: SoccerTutor.com Limited © 2016. All Rights Reserved.

All rights reserved. No part of this publication may be reproduced, stored in a retrieval system, or transmitted in any form or by any means, electronic, mechanical, photocopy, recording or otherwise, without prior written permission of the copyright owner. Nor can it be circulated in any form of binding or cover other than that in which it is published and without similar condition including this condition being imposed on a subsequent purchaser.

Author
Tag Lamche © 2016

Edited by
Alex Fitzgerald - SoccerTutor.com

Cover Design by
Alex Macrides, Think Out Of The Box Ltd.
Email: design@thinkootb.com Tel: +44 (0) 208 144 3550

Diagrams
Diagram designs by SoccerTutor.com. All the diagrams in this book have been created using SoccerTutor.com Tactics Manager Software available from *www.SoccerTutor.com*

Note: While every effort has been made to ensure the technical accuracy of the content of this book, neither the author nor publishers can accept any responsibility for any injury or loss sustained as a result of the use of this material.

COACH PROFILE: TAG LAMCHE

TAG LAMCHE

tag1football@gmail.com

CREDENTIALS:

- **UEFA 'A' COACHING LICENCE (PART 1)**

- **UEFA 'B' COACHING LICENCE**

- **M.PHIL DEGREE IN SPORTS COACHING (EDUCATION)**
  Master of Philosophy Post-Graduate Research Degree from Birmingham University (UK). The research focused on visual and cognitive skills in football.

- **FA YOUTH AWARD**

PREVIOUS & CURRENT COACHING ROLES:

- **4 YEARS COACHING EXPERIENCE AT A PROFESSIONAL FOOTBALL ACADEMY IN THE UK (OXFORD UNITED)**

- **SPECIALIST VISUAL SKILLS COACH (FOOTBALL)**

  Specialist technical coach who delivers workshops focused on improving perceptual and cognitive skills in football. Tag has delivered workshops and presentations at numerous UK professional clubs, including Chelsea FC, Crystal Palace FC, Leicester City FC, Middlesborough FC, Fulham FC and Everton FC amongst many others.

- **SPECIALIST COACH AND CONSULTANT TO THE BRITISH OLYMPIC ASSOCIATION (2007-2010)**

  Head of Sensory-Motor Skills BOA Elite Performance Programme

  Tag worked as a specialist coach and consultant for the British Olympic Association, helping pilot their Elite Performance Programme, working as one of a group of ten specialist coaches brought together from around the world by Sir Clive Woodward (England's World Cup winning rugby coach and the BOA's Elite Performance Director).

  Tag has also worked with a number of world class athletes in other professional sports such as tennis, judo, golf and skiing.

- **PLAYMAKER WORKSHOP LEADER/ PERCEPTUAL SKILLS COACH**

  Tag leads weekly academy workshops assisting players to develop advanced motor-visual skills to help improve performance in football. The workshops combine specific motor-visual skills training with a structured course in advanced ball mastery, using techniques and tactics derived from Futsal.

CONTENTS

CHAPTER 3: THE FINISHING PHASE 80

INTRODUCTION

This book hopes to deliver exactly what it says on the cover! First and foremost it is a technical and practical guide. My goal is to assist coaches and players committed to the philosophy of possession football based on playing out from the keeper and "through the thirds". I have yet to find a truly useful book dedicated to achieving this philosophy where the focus is on youth development. What follows is my attempt to redress this lack of reliable information. My approach is to first give positive examples of key patterns of play. I then recommend practices that can help you and your team achieve these on the field of play.

My aim is to provide numerous practical examples of how you can coach your players to play constructive football "building up play from the keeper".

Some coaches may wish to adopt the whole integrated approach as set out here, and others may prefer simply to cherry-pick the ideas they like best.

Every tactic and practice suggested in this book has been fully tried and tested. Furthermore, all the likely problems and challenges you may face when implementing these ideas are described and specific solutions are then suggested. This is another feature that distinguishes this book and should, I hope, make it a truly useful resource to coaches and players. It's vital to have a philosophy, but it's equally vital to know how to turn that philosophy into reality. And to succeed with this, you need good tactical options for every given situation. That's what this book sets out to provide, so your team will always have alternate ways to keep possession and advance the play. Furthermore, if and when things don't go to plan, you'll know what to do, and be confident to suggest strong alternatives to help your team "turn it around". Without this, it's amazing how quickly coaches are likely to abandon their ideals or simply accept paying lip-service to them.

With attention to detail and a positive attitude in practice, this tactical and technical guide should be all you need to get your team playing out from the back and through the thirds. As a coach, I am committed to sharing this knowledge in the name of encouraging possession based, attacking football.

Like all coaches I've got my insights from many different sources – other coaches, analysing games, reading books, watching videos etc. In football as in life, it all comes down to interpretation and what you want to achieve. Hence, what follows is how I've personally taken on and adapted what I've learnt, for better or worse. Having said that, I owe a debt of gratitude to a lot of people who have helped me along the coaching pathway. First and foremost to Enrique Guillen who proved a great mentor to me working together at a professional football academy for three years. The midfield rotations, the so-called 'Cut' and 'The X' are all movements I learnt to apply through working with Enrique. In addition, I'd like to thank Clive Woodward for his extended support and encouragement with my football awareness training programme and getting me started on my UEFA badges. Also to Brendon Rogers, Gareth Southgate, Frank Arnesen, Colin Calderwood, John Harbin, Iain Dowie, Damien Roden, Simon Clifford, Dave Billows, Les Taylor and Jim Kelman all of whom, in various ways, have helped or encouraged me along the coaching pathway, opening doors and providing positive feedback.

The overall purpose of this book is to share powerful and practical tactics and techniques for the benefit of all coaches and players committed to possession football and the beautiful game. I hope you enjoy the ride and get something from it.

Any feedback let me know by e-mail:
tag1football@gmail.com

WHY EXPLORE THIS APPROACH?

This book assumes a 4-3-3 or 4-2-3-1 team formation. However, a number of the fundamental movement patterns presented here are highly adaptable and can be modified to any formation you chose to play with. Although targeted at youth development level e.g. 12-16 years old, the practices set out can be adapted for younger as well as older players, including senior team players. If not the whole system, then certainly you should find a number of coaching ideas you can use or adapt from the many fundamental movement patterns and practices included. Alternatively, for those who just wish to deepen their understanding of football at a tactical and technical level, there should also be a lot for you to enjoy and get out of this book.

The philosophy of play outlined in *this book is based on the idea that it is better to have the ball than not have the ball*. However, to earn that right, you need to ensure your team is always empowered with a number of different options or movement patterns they can reliably use. In this way, they can have the confidence to "keep possession" and advance the play, looking to use their creativity to create scoring opportunities. It sounds simple enough - which is why we love football - but within that simplicity there is a lot of exciting stuff to learn.

The philosophy of play underlying the practices set out in this book involves:

1. *A commitment to "playing out" from the keeper*, that is, through coaching players to use effective patterns of play to advance the ball along the ground from the keeper and up the pitch.

2. *Advancing with good possession using well coordinated movement patterns* through 4 phases of play:

   - The Build-up Phase
   - The Consolidation Phase
   - The Incision Phase
   - The Finishing Phase

3. While the philosophy and the practices recommended in this book may appear highly structured, there is a vital proviso. As well as being structured, the idea is to present players with a rich variety of options or tactical tools they can explore. In this way you *empower players to make their own decisions - individually and collectively - as well as*

encouraging them to use their own creativity and natural attributes to best apply the ideas in practice. This ensures even more variety in terms of options for playing attractive attacking football. As the team become more accustomed to using the tactics set out here, they will get stronger and quicker at combining and progressing the play, looking to score.

4. The "set pieces" presented (e.g. corners and free-kicks) reinforce the philosophy of play:

Can we maintain possession of the ball as much as possible through coordinated movement patterns?

USING THIS BOOK TO ASSIST YOUR COACHING

For every practice, I've set out clear coaching points you can make with specific challenges you can set players both individually and as a group. So, typically, I will use the phrase "can the player" or "try" when outlining a challenge. This is to assist the coach in setting out the ideas in a way that is easily understandable for the players e.g. "can you run with the ball if you have space?" By phrasing challenges in this way, you clarify the goal, while empowering and motivating your players to explore it and achieve success.

A note about the structure of this book: I will look at a specific topic (e.g. how to play out from the back) in the following way. Firstly, I will give an overview of the key challenges involved. Whether you're a coach or a player, you need to understand why you're doing something. By first presenting the bigger picture, you help secure everyone's buy-in and motivation. So, I often refer to how a specific tactic or movement pattern will likely play out in a competitive game. Once you see how it could work in the full-blooded reality that is football, it will help you deliver the specific coaching session. Also, it will help you "see" the movement patterns as they evolve in competitive games.

As well as the game-related practices set out, I provide detailed commentary. In my opinion, too many coaching books fail the learner when it comes to providing more practical information. For example, what can the coach try when tactics go wrong or prove difficult in practice? To actually succeed with implementing a new approach or, indeed, any more involved tactical plans, you will always encounter problems and set-backs. This is where a lot of coaches might give up. They'll conclude, "Oh, it's just not possible with this group of players", or, for example, "we like to play out from the back, but only when it's on" etc.. And, of course, it rarely is "on" especially if you're only tactic is to ask your centre backs or full backs to "drop to receive". The reality is, your opponents will rarely sit back and give you the time to do this and to "build out". So, with limited knowledge of the many options available, coaches will too easily give up before they've even properly started. Likely result: Keeper kicks it long 80% of the time and everyone settles back to watch a dog's breakfast of a game served up with no team fully able to dominate the play. In grass-roots football this is arguably the default reality, certainly in the UK, although, no doubt, there are notable exceptions.

This book presents an alternative set of possibilities, outlining a tactical approach to football that favours the use of exciting and coordinated patterns of play. In my

experience, this approach provides the best platform for encouraging the individual creativity of your players.

Finally, a lot of coaching books assume that coaches have a full pitch available and a large squad of 20+ players. This book assumes a more realistic scenario with most practices designed for a squad of 14 players or less. It also assumes a half-pitch practice area (or smaller) to assist player learning. Most practices can also be easily adapted to occasions where you have fewer players e.g. 10 or 11. You can use a "neutral" or "magic" player when numbers are uneven. You can set a condition for "a one-touch" finish to free your keepers to play outfield and develop their game skills. Or you can position two cones half a yard inside either post and set a condition: To score, players must finish between the cone and the post. For those with larger squads and a full pitch, again, with a bit of imagination and planning, you can adapt the practices to suit the needs of your players.

DIAGRAM KEY

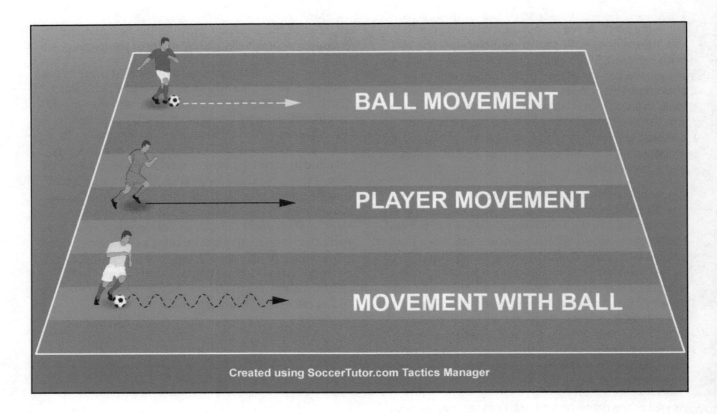

Created using SoccerTutor.com Tactics Manager

TACTICAL FORMAT

Each tactical situation includes clear diagrams with supporting notes such as:

- Name of Game Situation

- Description of Game Situation

- Tactical Instructions (if applicable)

PRACTICE FORMAT

Each practice includes clear diagrams with supporting training notes such as:

- Name / Objective of Practice

- Practice Organisation

- Variation or Progression (if applicable)

- Coaching Points

THE 4 PHASES OF COMBINATION PLAY

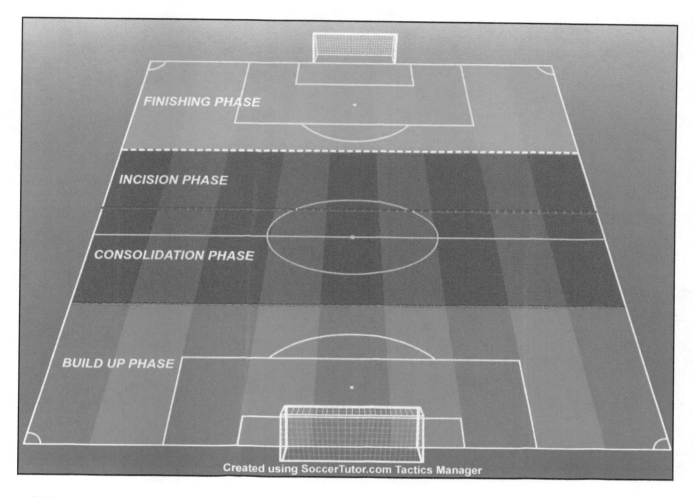

I. BUILD UP PHASE:

Where the team in possession look to coordinate their movements and combine passes to play out from their penalty area. Key players involved here are the keeper, the back four and the midfield three.

2. CONSOLIDATION PHASE:

Where the team in possession bring the ball out beyond their box and over the halfway line. In this next phase the two wingers and the striker also become involved.

3. INCISION PHASE:

Where the team in possession look to get beyond the defensive lines of their opponents with penetrating passes supported by good movement.

4. FINISHING PHASE:

Where the team in possession, having penetrated their opponent's back-line, look to finish off goal scoring opportunities.

FORMATION

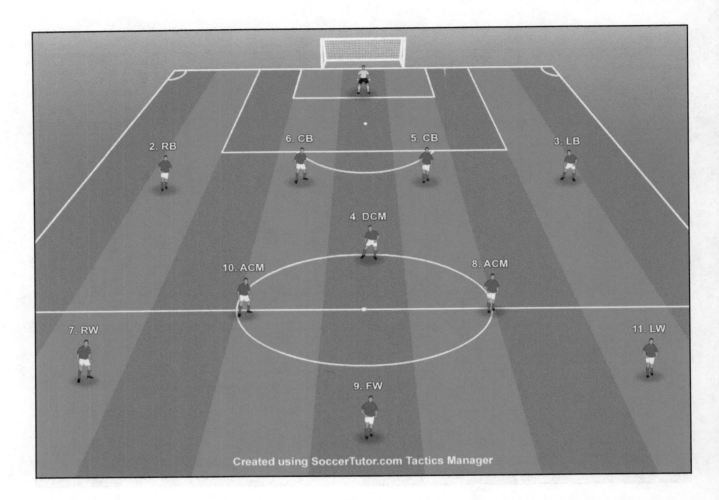

* For the examples in the first part of this book, we have used the 4-3-3 formation, but you can adapt all the movement patterns and practices to suit the formation of your team.

CHAPTER 1
THE BUILD UP & CONSOLIDATION PHASE

* For the examples in this chapter we have used the 4-3-3 formation, but you can adapt all the movement patterns and practices to suit the formation of your team.

BASIC SHAPE & MOVEMENT PATTERNS

Basic Set Up: The Starting Positions of the Back 4

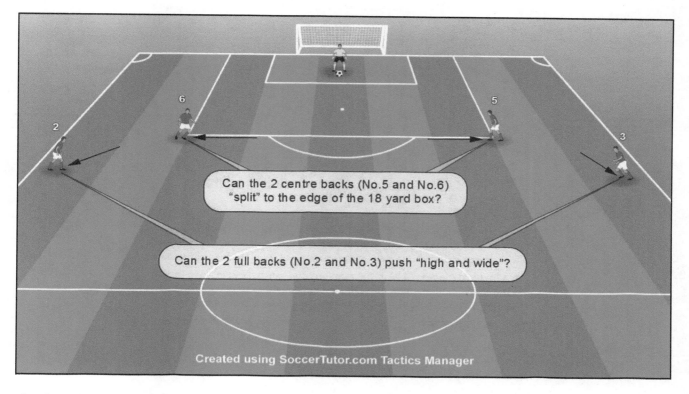

The above diagram shows the basic starting positions from a goal kick or with the keeper in possession. Anytime the keeper receives the ball and has both time and space available, can the back 4 be quick to "open up" along these lines?

The basic shape is as follows:

- Can the 2 centre backs (No.5 and No. 6) "split" to the edge of the 18 yard box?

- Can the 2 full backs (No.2 and No.3) push "high and wide"? That means the full backs should position themselves so they "hug the line" and prepare themselves in advance of the centre backs.

Coaching Point

Can your body position remain "half-turned" so you can see the ball and the rest of the pitch ahead?

Basic Set Up: Preparing the Midfield 3

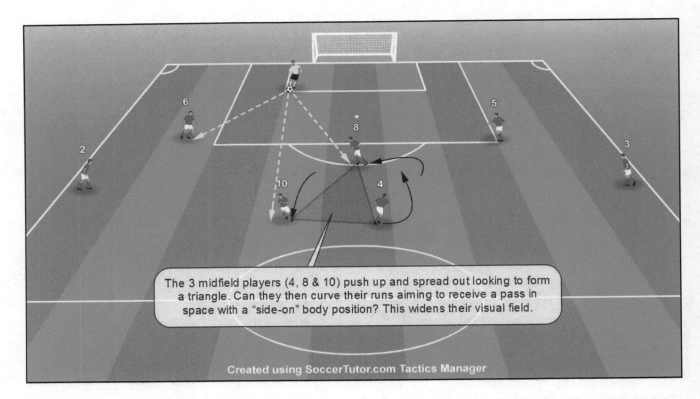

The 3 midfield players (4, 8 & 10) push up and spread out looking to form a triangle. Can they then curve their runs aiming to receive a pass in space with a "side-on" body position? This widens their visual field.

Created using SoccerTutor.com Tactics Manager

The 3 midfield players (No.'s 4, 8 and 10) function as the heart of the tactical system presented in this book. These 3 players and their coordinated movements drive the show. With the back-line positioned as before, *can these 3 midfielders look to form a triangle?* In forming this triangle, it's vital these 3 players also "push up" to create space well in front of the 18 yard box in preparation for the keeper's goal kick (or pass if it is in open play).

The trigger for the midfield rotation is when the keeper looks up ready to play the ball.

- Can the midfield 3 try to curve their runs into this created space?

- If they lose their markers, can they look to receive a pass either directly from the keeper or via the centre back?

By curving their runs (e.g. No. 8 in diagram), the midfielders will be better placed to receive the ball side-on. This will help them to turn and drive forward with the ball (if in space).

Alternatively, if under pressure, can they look to "bounce" (1 touch pass) the ball diagonally to the full back (No.2 or 3) or, better still, into the winger (No.7 or 11)?

By curving his run, the player widens his visual field and thereby improves his capacity to see opponents arriving to press him from behind (a very likely probability in this area!). This is what is meant by the phrase "open body position" as used in this book.

Midfield Rotation: Coordinated Movement Patterns

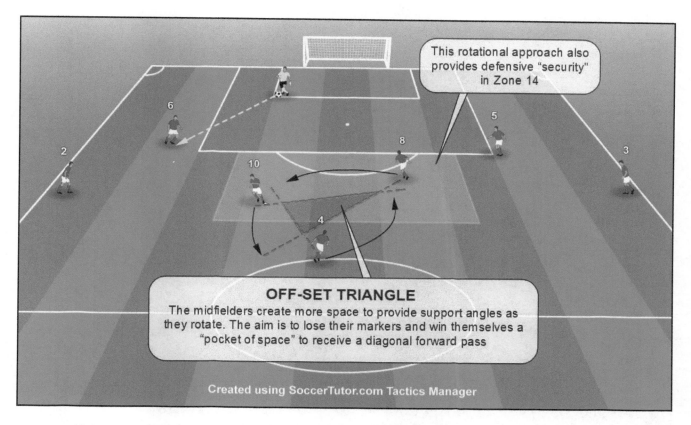

This rotational approach also provides defensive "security" in Zone 14

OFF-SET TRIANGLE

The midfielders create more space to provide support angles as they rotate. The aim is to lose their markers and win themselves a "pocket of space" to receive a diagonal forward pass

Created using SoccerTutor.com Tactics Manager

- Can the triangle formed by the 3 midfield players be off-set?

The red lines in the diagram show an ideal shape for the rotating midfield 3. So, for example, when playing out to the right, can the triangle the players form be off-set to the right and vice-versa when playing out to the left?

- Can the 3 midfield players show discipline and focus in achieving this challenge?

By off-setting the triangle as shown, *the midfielders create more space to provide a support angle as they rotate*. The aim, of course, is for them to lose their markers and win themselves a "pocket of space" to receive a diagonal forward pass (e.g. from the centre back No. 6 in the diagram).

As noted, it is vital the 3 midfield players maintain an "open body position" as they rotate so they can always see their teammate with the ball. As they do so, they must also try and maintain an effective distance from the ball and their teammates (see positioning of No.'s 6, 2 and 10 in the diagram).

- Can the midfielders keep creating clear triangles relative to the ball, looking to receive a pass in a "pocket of space"?

To achieve success with this, it is important the rotating midfielders (e.g. No. 8 in the diagram) *retain their shape and spin out at the correct distance. On occasions where the pass is NOT "on", it is vital that the rotating midfielder spin away, opening the space for the next midfielder to arrive.*

When a player receives a pass in space, they should look to turn and play forward. If, however, their run is tracked by an opponent, can they "bounce" the ball (first time pass) to the full back (e.g. No. 2), or play a diagonal forward pass to the winger who should be positioned further up the pitch?

The strength of *this rotational approach is that it also provides defensive "security"* in the central area in front of the box ("zone 14" as it's sometimes called). This can be seen in the diagram above, from the way the No.4 rotates his position to arrive centrally in front of the 2 centre backs with an "open" body shape. This helps provide protection in this vital and vulnerable zone, in the event possession is lost to opponents e.g. through a misplaced pass. If this happens, the 2 centre backs will also want to "tuck in" quickly. This will ensure defensive compactness with the full backs also dropping back to provide further cover and balance.

The Transition from the Build Up Phase to the Consolidation Phase

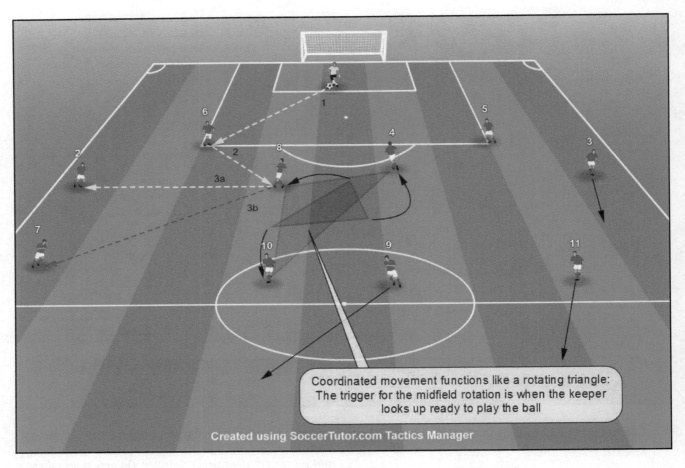

Coordinated movement functions like a rotating triangle:
The trigger for the midfield rotation is when the keeper
looks up ready to play the ball

Created using SoccerTutor.com Tactics Manager

This diagram shows the basic coordinated movements of the midfield.

This coordinated movement functions like a rotating triangle. This is how I describe it to my players to help them understand and see the bigger picture. The diagram also shows a few of the basic passing options available to the centre back (No.6 in the diagram) as he "opens up" to receive from the keeper. Notice the triangles created by the rotation of the midfield 3. The No.6 can play out wide to the right back (No.2) or into the path of the rotating No.8 (as shown in the diagram) or, if possible, up to the No.10.

The trigger for the midfield rotation is when the keeper looks up ready to play the ball. If the No.8 or No.4's run is NOT tracked by opponents, then our keeper also has the option of passing into these players. For this reason, once again, it's vital that our midfield players "arc their runs" across so they are positioned "side-on" to receive with a good view of the rest of the pitch. They can then turn and advance with the ball or play a first-time pass ("bounce pass" into a supporting wide player) e.g. from No.6 to No.8 to No. 2 or No.7 as shown in the diagram.

- Meanwhile, can the keeper try to provide a good support angle behind the ball for a back pass?

- When opponents press intensely and the keeper receives a back-pass, can he look to spread the play wide with a driven or lofted pass?
(This will be further explored in this section)

Passing Options of Rotating Midfield 3

Consolidation Phase: Midfielders and Wide Players Combine

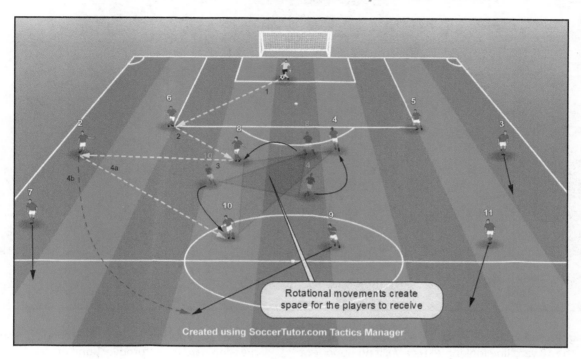

Rotational movements create space for the players to receive

Created using SoccerTutor.com Tactics Manager

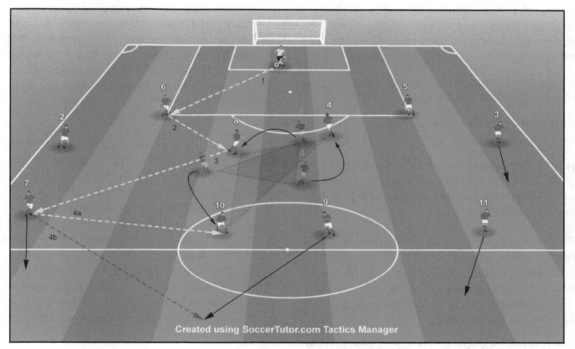

Created using SoccerTutor.com Tactics Manager

These two diagrams show the basic rotational movements of the midfield 3 and subsequent passing options. The starting positions are represented by the transparent players. When these rotational movements create space for the players to receive, chances are there will be pressure from opponents closing them down. As we will see, it is therefore important to coach your players to use "bounce" passes (1 touch) or quickly use 2 touches - control and pass.

The diagrams show examples of a midfielder (No. 8 in diagram) passing first time to No.2 / No.7. These wide supporting players can then look to play diagonal passes for the forward runs of the rotating No.10 or, alternatively, lofted passes or driven ground passes through a channel and into the path of the No.9 who makes a diagonal run, as shown.

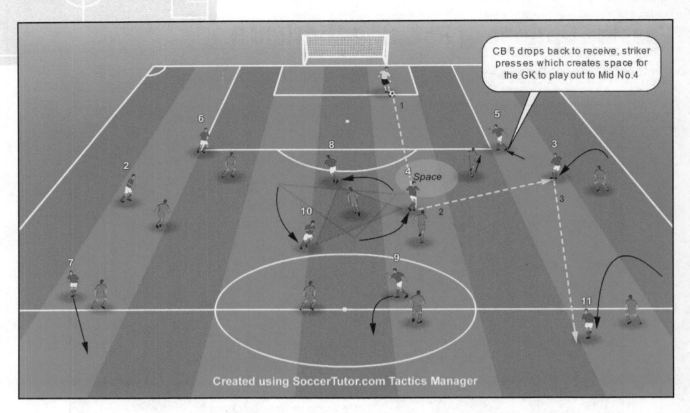

CB 5 drops back to receive, striker presses which creates space for the GK to play out to Mid No.4

Space

Created using SoccerTutor.com Tactics Manager

This diagram shows another option. A centre back drops back to the 18 yard line looking to receive. If no opponent closes him down, the keeper can look to play into him while the other players make supporting movements. However, if the opposition striker presses the centre back, this opens up a space and opportunity to play out.

- *Can the midfield 3 rotate and can the keeper play into the No.4 as he drops into the space created?*

- *Can the No.4 arrive with his body half-turned to receive the pass?*

- *If an opponent presses the No.4, can the full back (e.g. No.3) look to make a well timed supporting run in front of his marker? If so, can the No.4 now play a first time pass to him?*

The No.3 can now either run forward with the ball if there is space or, otherwise, look to "ping a pass" into a forward "running the channel" (e.g. No. 11 in the diagram). Failing this, *the No.4, if highly pressed, can simply "set" the ball back to the keeper who should position himself so he is available to receive the back pass.*

- Can the keeper now look for his back-line to quickly "reload" in terms of their shape and the team try another coordinated movement together?

- When the keeper is pressed by an on-rushing opponent, can he look to strike a long diagonal lofted pass into No.7 or No. 11? This option can be effective when done with precision. Indeed, *the "set" ball is easier to strike long, especially for younger players.*

Also, as the opponent team will likely be pushed up pressing hard for a "turnover", one precise long ball can eliminate a number of opponents and trigger a quick and dangerous counter attack down the flank. Take note, that in situations like this, *it is vital you coach your keeper to clearly target the wingers*. This is a much safer option than the keeper simply kicking it up the middle of the pitch, where the opposition are likely to win the ball, which could leave your team very exposed in central areas.

These are just some of the many variations that are possible, allowing your team to be flexible and creative in exploring ways to play out from the keeper. We will look at more examples shortly, extending from the build-up to the consolidation phase of play. Firstly however, I want to suggest a few key exercises you can use with your players to introduce them to the basic shape and movement patterns involved. These exercises are easy to set up and easy for players to understand. Given a bit of practice with these, your players will start to see the shape and rotations clearly. This will give them the confidence to go out and explore them against opponents in competitive games.

Rotation of the Midfield 3 in a Pass & Move Practice (Unopposed)

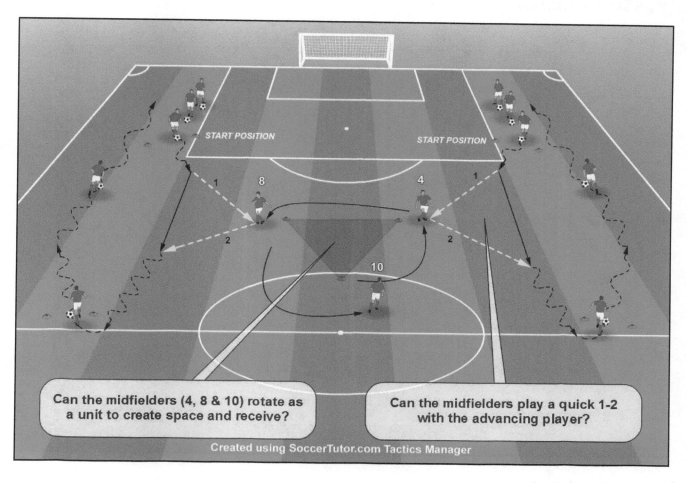

Can the midfielders (4, 8 & 10) rotate as a unit to create space and receive?

Can the midfielders play a quick 1-2 with the advancing player?

Created using SoccerTutor.com Tactics Manager

Practice Organisation

Using half a full sized pitch, we mark out the cones in the positions shown. We have 3 midfielders positioned by 3 cones in the middle which form a triangle. All other players have a ball each and the practice starts with the players running forward with the ball on both sides simultaneously. Most players start behind the first cone gate with one player starting on the halfway line to keep the players and practice moving.

The players need to show good awareness running with the ball, before then playing a one-two combination with one of the 3 midfield players who rotate after each pass (anti-clockwise in diagram). Once the midfielder "bounces" the ball back (1 touch pass), can the players run at speed with the ball toward the halfway line where they turn and run back to the starting gate? Rotate the midfield 3 players.

Coaching Points

1. Can you make *well timed movements*?
2. Can you *weight your passes correctly* into a player or into his path to run onto?
3. Can you provide good communication e.g. a clear hand signal pointing where you want the pass delivered?
4. Can you use visual signals for where you want the pass?
5. Can the *3 rotating midfielders retain a good triangular shape*?
6. Can midfielders (if pressed) play a "first time" pass while having a *good open body shape*?
7. Can midfielders *"arc their runs"* across as they rotate to receive a pass? This will help them maintain a good body shape and also *ensure "security" is maintained* in the key central defensive area in case possession is lost.
8. Can all players *play with good anticipation, composure and with their heads up*?

PROGRESSION
Rotation of the Midfield 3 in a Pass & Move Practice (Passive Pressure)

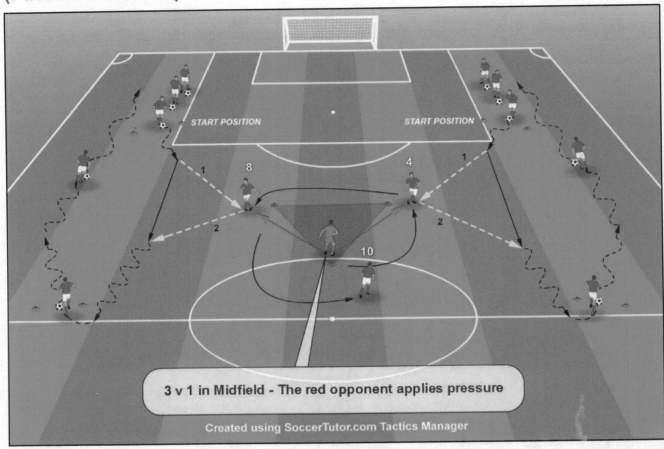

3 v 1 in Midfield - The red opponent applies pressure

Created using SoccerTutor.com Tactics Manager

Practice Organisation

This is a progression of the previous practice and we add one *"PASSIVE" opponent* (red player) to press the midfield 3 as they move to receive the ball. Defending passively means that the red player should not actively try and intercept any passes or attempt to tackle the midfielder receiving the ball. Instead he should simply "track" the run (i.e. run close behind as if pressing) as the midfielders look to play "bounce" passes (1 touch) out wide. Rotate the 3 midfield players.

Progressions

1. As the players develop and improve, add a second passive opponent to provide additional pressure.
2. Once a good rhythm is established, make the opponents press the midfielders harder i.e. not fully competitive but almost looking to tackle or intercept passes.
3. Once the players are showing good ability, make both opponents fully active. They press and try to intercept passes into the 3 rotating midfielders.

Coaching Points

1. Can the 3 midfielders coordinate their movements with well timed runs, looking to receive passes while maintaining a strong triangular shape?
2. Can midfielders be on the half-turn for the incoming ball so they are well positioned to play a first time pass?
3. Can midfielders explore their technique for receiving passes while shielding the ball from the opponent?
4. Can the other players check away from their marker to create space to receive the pass?
5. Can all players weight their passes effectively into the path of the runs from their teammates?
6. Can you successfully communicate where you want the pass delivered i.e. using hand signals, pointing where you want the pass?

PROGRESSION
Rotation of the Midfield 3 in a Pass & Move Practice: Passing to the Advanced Midfielder

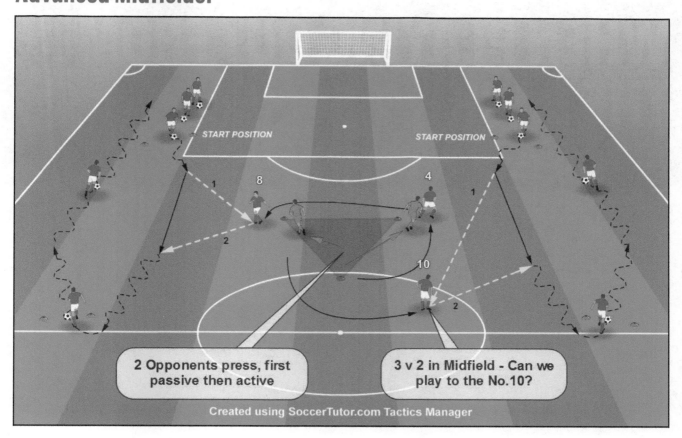

START POSITION   START POSITION

2 Opponents press, first passive then active

3 v 2 in Midfield - Can we play to the No.10?

Created using SoccerTutor.com Tactics Manager

Practice Organisation

This progression is the same as the previous practice but we add a challenge for the players: Can you, when possible, play a pass into the more advanced midfielder? (No.10 in diagram)

The 2 red opponents apply passive pressure to start. In the diagram example, the more advanced midfielder (No.10) times his run to receive in the space cleared by the deepest midfielder's movement (No.4 in diagram). He then plays a first time pass ("bounce") back into the space for the oncoming teammate to receive and continue his run.

Progressions

Once the players are performing the practice successfully the majority of the time and a good rhythm is established, make both red opponents fully active. They press and try to intercept passes into the 3 rotating midfielders.

Coaching Points

1. Can the more advanced midfielder (No.10 in diagram) time his "arced run" to arrive in space and play a first time pass?
2. Can the players running with the ball pass using good technique, driving the ball forward along the ground into the run of the more advanced of the 3 midfielders?
3. Emphasise that the first pass needs to have "ping" and by keeping the ball on the ground, it is easier to execute a quick one-two as shown in the diagram.
4. If the pass is played beyond the nearest teammate (e.g. beyond the rotating midfield No. 4 in the diagram), the pass is a better, more attacking option.

    A pass to No.4 can be seen as a "first option pass", as he is the nearest teammate, whereas the pass to the more advanced No.10 is a "second option" pass as this player is in a more advanced position.

TEAM SHAPE & ROTATIONS WHEN PLAYING OUT FROM THE BACK

Team Shape When Playing Out from the Back: Triangles & Diamonds

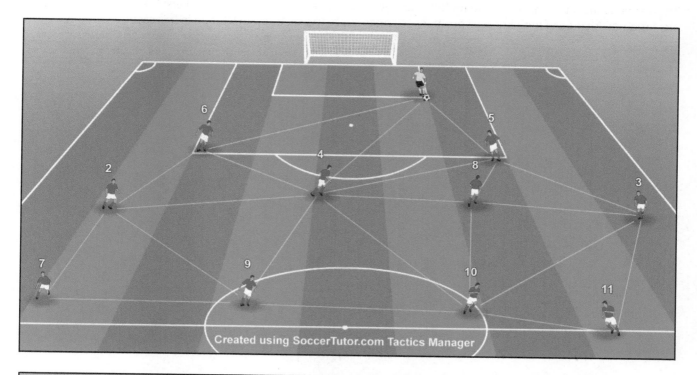

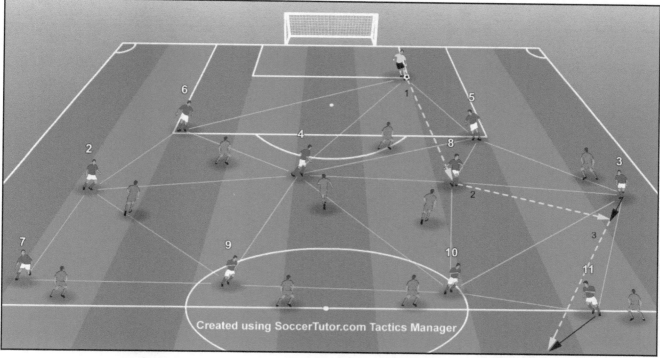

Here is an overview of the team's attacking shape as they prepare to play out from the back. The first diagram shows the team without opponents and the second shows the team facing high pressing opponents.

1.   The distances between the players should be consistent and maintained.
2.   The triangles and rhombus (diamond) shapes must be established.

3. The correct width and depth should be created.

4. There should be space for good mobility, especially in the central areas.

5. The "open" / "side on" body positions should be relative to the position of the ball.

The diagrams show the importance of mobility (rotations) in the central areas to lose markers. There is lots more about increasing the degree of mobility in all positions to create space to play through later on in this section.

Exploring the Second Option Pass

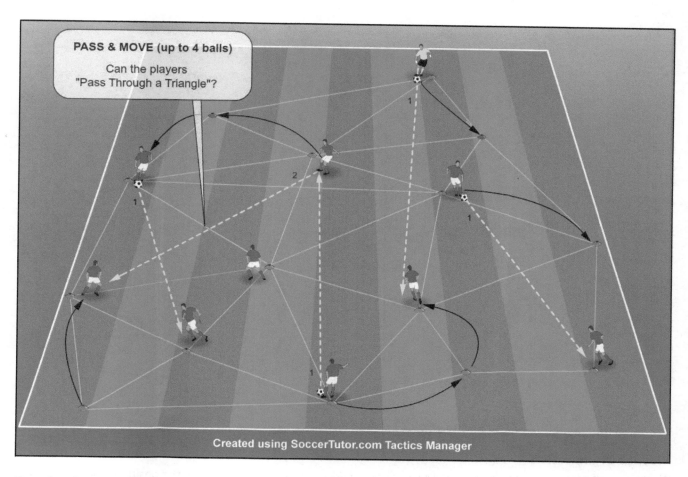

PASS & MOVE (up to 4 balls)

Can the players
"Pass Through a Triangle"?

Created using SoccerTutor.com Tactics Manager

Practice Organisation

Using half a pitch, we mark out cones 10 yards apart to form a network of triangles. Start with 1 or 2 balls and progress to using 4 balls. Start by giving a clear demo of what a "first option pass" looks like (e.g. to the nearest player). Set players the challenge to see if they can "pass and move" between the cones using a maximum of 2 touches ("control and pass") to play a "first option pass" into the nearest teammate.

Depending on the number of players, you can use "rolling subs" if necessary. Can they communicate with teammates to come on in their place? If a player doesn't receive a pass within 3 seconds they should move to a new free position.

Progressions

1. Add 2 passive opponents who simply move around to block passing channels.
2. Once players show understanding and ability with this practice, show them what a "second option pass" is.
    Can you make the players aware that the challenge now is to pass to the player beyond the nearest teammate?
    Can they, where possible, play a pass "through a triangle" into the "second-option" player?
    That is, NOT to the nearest teammate but, if possible, into the more advanced player (or a player arriving beyond).

Coaching Points

1. Can you practice losing your marker? They should check away before moving to receive.
2. Can you time your runs to arrive into a free space and receive a pass?
3. Can you successfully communicate where you want the pass delivered i.e. using hand signals, pointing where you want the pass?
4. Can you "ping" your second option passes along the ground? (Easier to control and pass the ball on quickly)

PROGRESSION
Position Specific Pass & Move Combinations

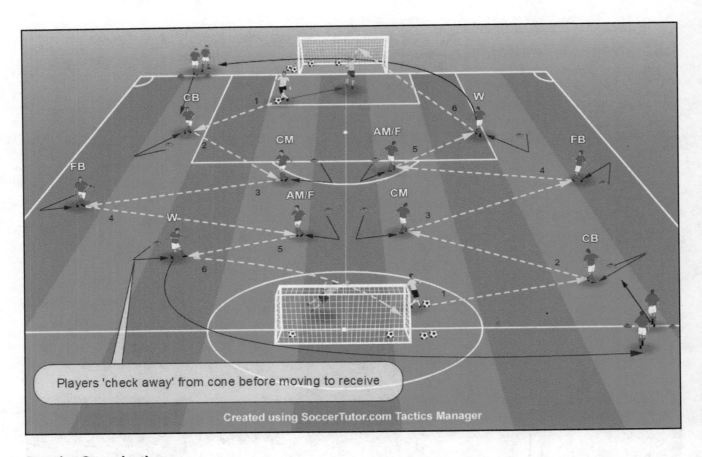

Players 'check away' from cone before moving to receive

Created using SoccerTutor.com Tactics Manager

Practice Organisation

We divide half a full sized pitch into 2 equal sections and mark out 5 cones in each half in the positions shown. We have 14 outfield players in this practice. There are also 2 full sized goals and 2 goalkeepers.

Both goalkeepers start the sequence at the same time with a pass to the centre back position (CB). The other cones represent the positions of a central midfielder (CM), a full back (FB), an attacking midfielder/forward (AM/F) and a winger (W).

The passing sequence is as shown in the diagram (1-5) and the players move to the next cone, following their pass. When the winger (W) receives a pass, he shoots at goal and then runs round to join the group on the other side. This is a continuous practice, working in an anti-clockwise direction.

The players should use a maximum of 2 touches ("control & pass") but you can adapt this depending on player ability. The players are positioned behind the cones and should check away from the cone (as shown) to receive on the move.

This practice benefits all the players as they get to explore the shape and movement needed from all the key positions on the pitch. This will help enhance their understanding and ability to visualise the pattern of play.

Coaching Points

1. Can you make well timed movements to create space (check away) and receive the pass?
2. Can you signal where you want the pass using clear communication?
3. Can you adopt a good half-turned body position to ensure you can see the full field of play?
4. Can you receive the ball showing good control and then deliver precise and weighted passes using good technique to comply with the 2 touch condition?

VARIATION / PROGRESSION
Position Specific Pass & Move Combinations with a Second Option Pass

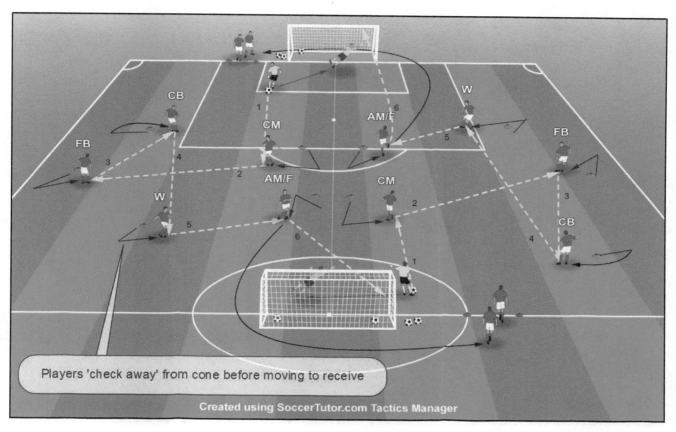

Players 'check away' from cone before moving to receive

Created using SoccerTutor.com Tactics Manager

Practice Organisation

In this variation of the previous practice, we change the passing sequences to allow for more variations and progressions. The players still follow their pass no matter what the sequence is.

You can start with the example shown in the diagram. The keeper passes to the central midfielder (CM) who drops back (side-on) and plays a "bounce" pass (1 touch) out wide to the full back (FB), and the full back sets the ball back to the centre back (CB). All of these passes are *first option passes* i.e. the option nearest to the player on the ball.

To explore *second option passing*, the centre back (3) then makes a more penetrating forward pass to the winger (W) as shown. The winger then sets the ball back to the attacking midfielder/forward (AM/F) who shoots at goal. The players rotate their positions and the AM/F runs round to join the group on the other side.

This unopposed practice allows players to explore key passing combinations based on the team shape. Can players establish an understanding and a team rhythm with well weighted passes and good movement? Once this is established, encourage players to explore different passing variations while maintaining the same dynamic shape.

Coaching Points

1. Challenge the players: Can you combine using first and, when possible, second option passes to build up play?

2. Can you make 2 movements (i.e. check away) prior to receiving the ball?
   This will instil a good habit of looking to create space against tight marking/pressing opponents.

3. Can you line up with the incoming pass, enabling you to play a first time pass?

4. Can you signal (using your arms) which foot (left or right) you want the ball played into?
   This increases the chances they will receive the ball where they want it. This will promote "first-time" passing skills.

5. Can you execute your passes with 'ping' and precision? Can you keep the ball on the ground?
   Look out for players who are struggling with this and give them technical guidance on how to deliver a crisp pass over 5/10/15/20 yards.

PROGRESSION
Position Specific Second Option Passing Combinations

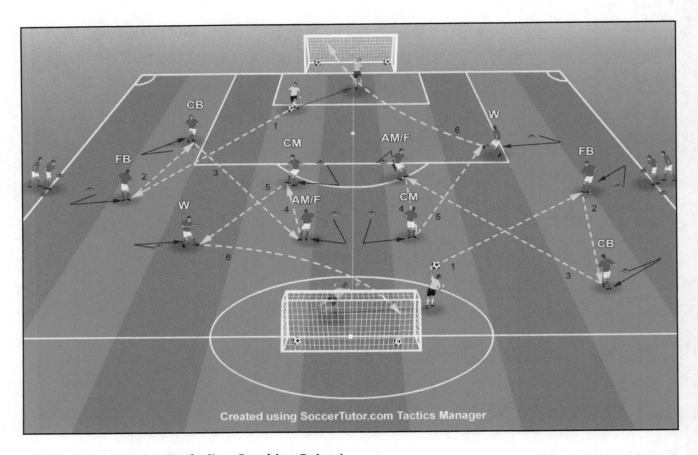

Created using SoccerTutor.com Tactics Manager

Practice Organisation (Including Coaching Points)

This progression is the same set up as the previous 2 practices but this time the starting gate is on the side of the pitch (blue gates in the diagram).

This is the same practice (pass and follow), however, in this progression, challenge the players to explore the following pattern of play:

1. Can the keeper play into the full back?
2. Can the full back check away before moving to receive (creating space) and then "set" the ball back to the player in the centre back role?
3. Can the player in the centre back role then play a penetrating "second option" pass into the forward?
4. Can the forward "set" the ball back to the supporting midfielder?
5. Can the midfielder then play into the winger as he cuts inside aiming to shoot on goal?

Although this pattern of play is shown as a variation of playing out from the keeper, its relevance with regard to quick combination play in the final third will become more apparent as we progress through this book.

Many of the movement patterns we explore are patterns aimed at assisting a team to play through pressure from the keeper are also useful in playing through opponents in more advanced areas of the pitch.

By coaching your team in numerous ways to play out from the back, you will also be coaching fundamental pass and move patterns relevant to the attacking and finishing phase. This is why coaching your players to effectively play out from the back has more general benefits.

PROGRESSION
Building Up Play from the Goalkeeper with Midfield Rotations in a Game Specific Practice

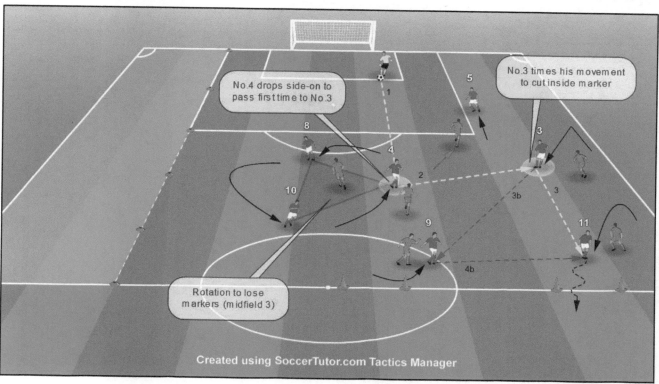

No.4 drops side-on to pass first time to No.3

No.3 times his movement to cut inside marker

Rotation to lose markers (midfield 3)

Created using SoccerTutor.com Tactics Manager

Practice Organisation

Using half a full sized pitch, we cone off the flank area and mark out 2 cone goals (3 yards wide) on the halfway line in the positions shown in the diagram. We play a 7 (+GK) v 6 game. The numbers can be adapted to how many players you have available.

The blue team have 1 centre back (5), 1 full back (3), 3 rotating midfielders (4, 8 & 10), 1 winger (11) and 1 striker (9).

The blue team start as they play out from the keeper and try to work the ball forward and then dribble the ball through one of the cone goals on the halfway line. If the ball goes out of play, resume the practice with a goal kick.

Variation: Cone off the opposite flank area, so the players practice building up play on the other side of the pitch.

Progressions

1. To start with, ask the opposition (reds) to play passively i.e. just closing down space and pressing without actively trying to win the ball. Once the blue players progress and a rhythm in possession is established, you can intensify the challenge and have the opponents apply full competitive pressure.

2. If the pressing team (reds) win the ball, they then have 10 seconds to score in the goal past the keeper. This increases the competitive element of the practice.

Coaching Points

1. Can the team play out from the back using good pass and move technique while maintaining strong triangular shapes?

2. Use a tactics board to help show the players how to build up play in this section of a full sized pitch, explaining specific patterns and the concept of first option and second option passes.

3. Can they perform the coordinated movements as set out on the tactics board?

PROGRESSION
Midfield Rotations to Build Up Play from the Goalkeeper in a Dynamic Game

Created using SoccerTutor.com Tactics Manager

Practice Organisation

Using half a full sized pitch, we mark out the cones in the positions shown in the diagram. There is a central box which is 25 x 20 yards. We have 1 full sized goal with a goalkeeper and 2 cone goals on the halfway line (3 yards wide). We play a 9 (+GK) v 6 game. The numbers can be adapted to how many players you have available.

The blue team have 2 centre backs (5 and 6), 2 full backs (2 and 3), 3 rotating midfielders (4, 8 & 10) and 2 wingers (7 and 11). The red cones near the flanks mark out the starting positions of the full backs and wingers. The reds have 2 strikers, 2 central midfielders and 2 wingers.

The practice starts with the blue team's goalkeeper and they aim to build up play and finally dribble the ball through one of the cone goals on the halfway line (1 point).

The blue midfielders start their rotations in the box with a 3 v 2 advantage. The aim is to pass to the spare midfielder who has created space to receive. The team can then combine to work the ball to the halfway line. An example of a passing combination is shown in the diagram. If the ball goes out of play, resume the practice with a goal kick.

Progressions

1. To start with, ask the opposition (reds) to play passively i.e. just closing down space and pressing high up the pitch without actively trying to win the ball. Once the players progress, you can intensify the challenge and have the opponents apply full competitive pressure.

2. If the pressing team (reds) win the ball, they then have 10 seconds to score in the goal past the keeper. This increases the competitive element of the practice.

Coaching Points

1. Can the team play out from the back using good pass and move technique?

2. Can the midfield 3 retain a triangle shape and make good movements to create space for one of them to receive?

3. Can the midfield players use a good body position and arc their runs, looking to receive side-on?

4. Can all players time their runs effectively to link up and play out?

Creating Space to Play Through Pressure: Centre Backs Tuck in & the Midfield 3 Rotate

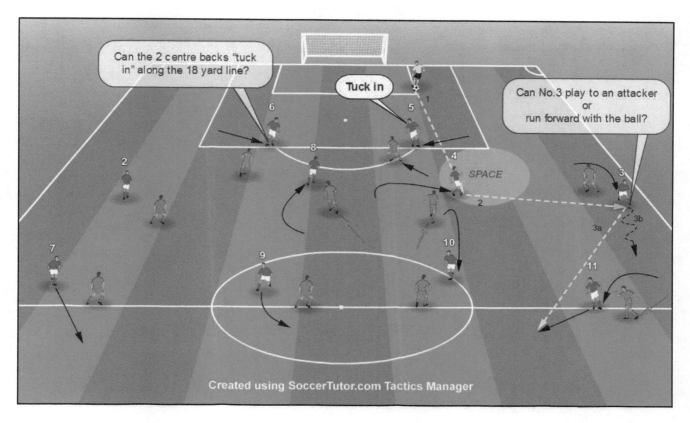

The key to success when playing out from the keeper is for your team to learn how to execute a number of variations. In this way, you stay one step ahead of your opponents. The idea is to leave them playing catch up, trying to second guess what you're going to do next.

Using the same 9 v 6 situation when building up play as in the previous practice game, here is another variation your team can explore to build out from the keeper.

- At a goal kick or when the keeper recovers possession, can the 2 centre backs "tuck in" along the 18 yard line?

- Can the 3 midfielders also tuck in, so they are no wider than the centre backs?

This will help create a potential channel for the keeper to then play into the rotating midfielders arriving into the space created wide of the centre back. If done effectively, with a well arced run, the midfielder could receive with space to advance with the ball.

Alternatively, if he receives but is closed down, he can "bounce" the ball (first time pass) to the full back (3) as shown in the diagram. Ideally, the full back will show good anticipation and start a "blind-side" forward run, looking to receive a diagonal forward pass beyond his

marker. He can then run forward with the ball or play a driven forward pass (along the ground or lofted) into the winger (11), No.10 or striker (9) who make runs in behind.

With regard to triggers, these are provided simply by the way players position themselves. So, in this example, the 2 centre backs would communicate verbally e.g. "Tuck in" or communicate through visual signals e.g. hand signals. The keeper would then position the ball wide along the 6 yard box and the rest of the team would understand what the coordinated movements would now likely be.

Creating Space to Play Through Pressure: 2 Centre Backs Drop & 2 Midfielders Split

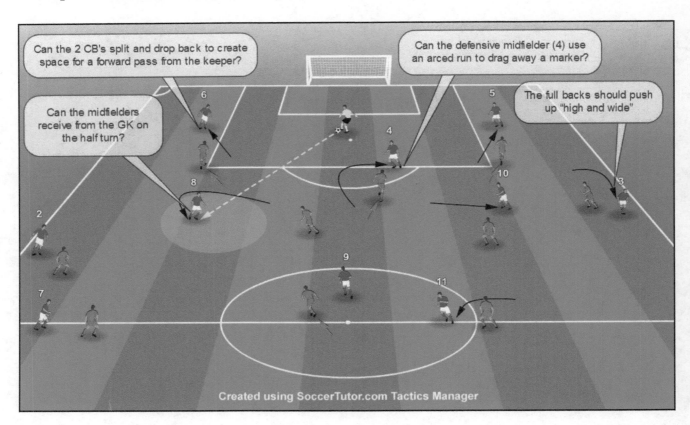

This variation is also effective for the team to play out from the keeper. If you're playing 3 at the back (e.g. 3-4-3 or 3-5-2) this can work well as it creates a lot of space for up to 5 players to receive a pass from the keeper.

- At a goal kick or receiving a pass back, can the keeper position himself at the centre of his 6 yard box?

This will maximise the number of potential passing channels available. Once the keeper has the ball centrally and looks up ready to play, this is the trigger for supporting players to make the coordinated movements. The full backs should push up "high and wide" and encourage the wingers to further "stretch the play" or look to come inside with an eye on running into a channel, aiming to receive a longer range pass.

- **TRIGGER:** When the keeper looks up and is ready to play, can the 2 centre backs (5 and 6) drop back with a side-on body position, looking to receive?

- As they do this, can the No.4 drop into the space created with a strong arcing run looking to receive side-on? It's vital that the No.4 push up first. This is so he has space to drop into, looking to receive or play a "bounce" pass (1 touch pass when pressed) around the edge of the box. If you're playing with 3 at the

back, then this movement would be made by your third centre back.

- As the 2 centre backs drop and the No.4 arcs his run in the space created, can the 2 attacking midfielders (8 and 10) split with a good side-on body position, looking to receive straight from the keeper?

The drop-off movement from the centre backs will likely draw in high pressing strikers, thereby creating space to play through the channel. If this movement is done well, the keeper should have up to 5 passing options to choose from. He can pass to either centre back if their runs are not tracked, or into the holding midfielder or, failing that, into either of the more attacking central midfielders.

- Can the keeper quickly assess which of these 5 options has the most space and best body position to receive, looking to advance the play?

- Can the keeper take the best option available and look to support his pass as well as possible?

(See practice on Pg. 47 'Goalkeeper Support Angles and Accurate Passing to Switch Play')

Drop & Split Continued: Variation

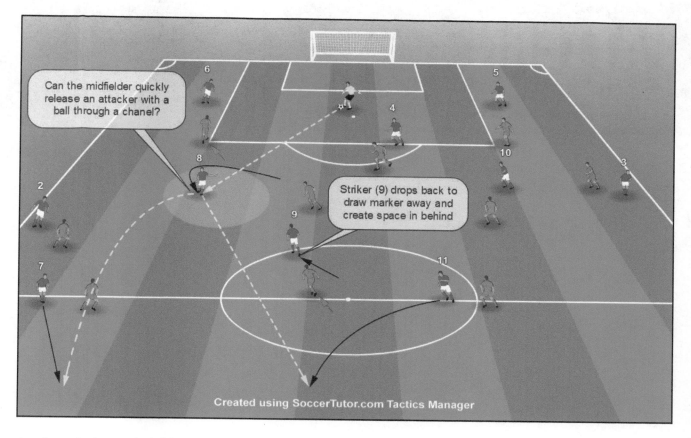

- Once the keeper has delivered his pass, can players quickly adjust their positioning to provide good support angles as well as promising outlets for a more attacking forward pass?

In this scenario, the striker (No.9) cleverly rotates his position with No.11 who has moved inside. Timing his run to beat the off-side trap, the No.11 receives a well weighted pass from No.8 into the space behind the opponent's defensive line. The striker (9) has made a simple decoy ("selfless") run to drag the red centre back away and create extra space for a diagonal driven pass into the path of the winger (11).

This is a good example of *Passing Through a Triangle into a Mobile Attacker*. The triangle in this scenario is made up of the passer (8), the right back (2) and the striker (9) who has dropped back towards the ball. Effectively, the No.8 has 2 very positive passing options:

1. A driven pass into the channel in time with No.11's diagonal run.

2. No.7 with a lofted ball "over the top".

3. Of course, there are many other possibilities that can open up using the drop and split movement as a way of playing out from the back. One of its distinct strengths is the way it can suck in a number of opponents pressing high up the pitch. This can leave the opposition short on numbers in central midfield and leave them vulnerable to quick incision play and overloads going forward. The key to success is for players to coordinate/sync their runs effectively.

- Can the players disguise where they are going to pass and play forward with precision and pace?

'THE CUT' MOVEMENT PATTERN

'The Cut': Basic Movement Pattern

'The Cut' is a fundamental movement pattern often seen in football and in numerous scenarios. In its basic form, it involves 2 players. However, it is a key trigger for a number of more complex patterns of play we will now explore. These can involve upwards of 4/5 players coordinating their movements. I will give a number of practical examples in this section. These are just a few of the numerous ways you and your players can practice playing out from the back.

More generally, the cut is very useful and versatile as a 2 man movement pattern to assist your players to play through pressure e.g. helping them create space to attack when they are tightly marked, in both wide and central areas. The more your players get to explore its basic forms, and try them against opponents, the better!

The cut is built on the basic starting shape as outlined for the back 4, plus the midfield 3 rotations. Combining these 3 elements into an integrated approach will provide your team with an almost limitless variety of ways to "play out".

For those wondering why to bother with all this "playing out the back" stuff, I will provide a number of examples of how a team can use these movement patterns to quickly and incisively "play through the thirds". From this platform, the team can then go on to create exciting goal scoring opportunities. The examples given only scratch the surface of the possibilities. No doubt you and your players, given time, will conceive of many more options you can put to good effect in helping you win football games in style through strong possession play.

The above diagram shows *'The Cut'* in its basic form with players in their starting positions as the keeper prepares to take a goal kick. The movement starts when the keeper looks up ready to play. The nearest centre back triggers the movement pattern by calling out *"Cut"* or whatever code your team prefer to adopt. The centre back then begins a diagonal forward run across and in front of the pressing opponent (see diagram on next page). As the centre back does this, the full back drops back down the line, looking to receive a pass from the keeper.

'The Cut' provides an exciting platform for numerous possible ways of initiating attacks. By exploring some of the options set out, your players will learn to advance through the thirds, enjoying strong possession.

By maintaining reasonable discipline and dynamic shape, your team has the potential to create countless passing options with plenty of scope for individual expression and creativity, including turning and running with the ball when possible.

Combining 'The Cut' with the Midfield 3 Rotations

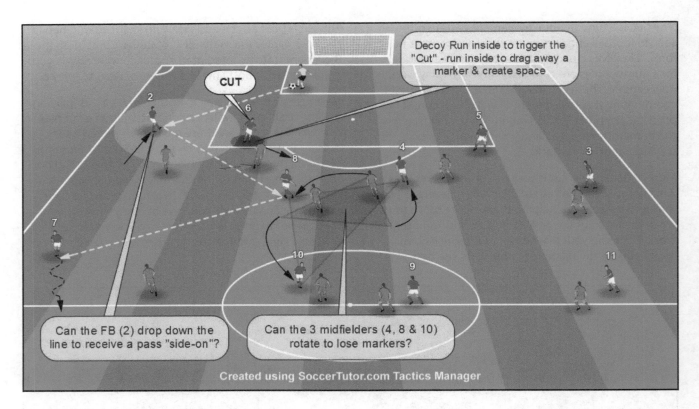

This is where it gets more interesting. By combining the basic *'Cut'* movement pattern with the midfield 3 rotations as shown in the diagram, your players will start to enjoy a huge variety of ways to play out from the keeper and through pressure.

All these basic patterns of play can be coached, using the step-by-step practices in this book. It's not rocket science, it's all doable! So why be content with your keeper simply kicking the ball up the field? This greatly limits the technical and tactical development of your players. Your defenders and midfielders end up like spectators watching the ball fly over their heads, and, more than likely, straight to the opposition. Similarly, if your team rely on only one or two ways of "playing out", it's very likely your opponents will soon suss you out and stop you in your tracks. Hence, it is vital to empower your team with a number of different options for playing out from the back. Even with just one hour training a week, some of the more basic movement patterns outlined here can be developed to good effect.

The diagram shows *'The Cut'* with the centre back tucking in to stand in front of the pressing opponent. He calls out *"Cut!"* (Or whatever code your team agree on) and runs diagonally across his opponent. If the opponent tracks the run, this triggers the movement of the full back (2) to drop back down the line, looking to receive a pass side-on.

Assuming this movement allows the full back (2) to lose his marker and he finds space to run into and receive, the keeper is open to pass to him. No.2 may be able to run forward with the ball. Alternatively, if he is being closed down, he can ping a pass "into the pocket" for the rotating and arriving midfielder (e.g. No. 8) who should ensure to "arc his run" as part of the rotation of the 3 midfielders. Assuming the opponents are pressing high and hard, the No. 8 can now look to play a first time pass out wide to No.7. As mentioned earlier, it is vital that the 3 midfielders maintain the correct distances as they rotate (10/15 yards apart in a triangle shape). If the pass from No.2 is *NOT* played, then the 3 midfielders (No.'s 4, 8 & 10) should 'Spin Out' and trigger another rotation.

With just 3 simple 10/15 yard passes, the team has created an exciting, coordinated pattern of play. They have the ball in good possession, with the No.7 crossing the halfway line, looking to attack at pace down the flank.

Don't forget all the movement patterns outlined in this book can he executed down BOTH flanks in all their variations. This effectively doubles the number of options available to your players for playing out from the back and through opponent pressure. It is vital that you therefore encourage your players to explore these patterns of play both down the right and the left flank.

'The Cut' Movement Pattern & Combination Play in a Game Specific Practice

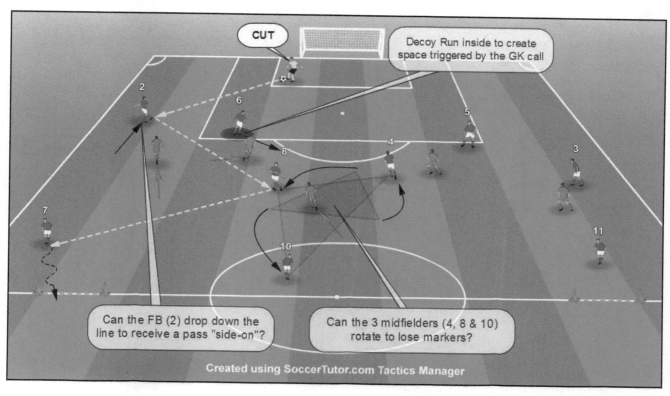

Practice Organisation

Using half a full sized pitch, we play a 9 (+GK) v 5 practice game. We have a full sized goal and 2 cone gates on the halfway line in the positions shown (3/4 yards wide). You can use cones or markers to show the start positions for the back 4, the midfield 3 and the 2 wingers if it is easier for the players.

The blue team play out from the keeper and their aim is to use 'The Cut' movement, combine and then dribble the ball through either of the cone gates. If the red team win the ball, they then have 10 seconds to try and score or we restart the practice with the keeper. If the ball goes out, we again restart the practice with the keeper.

The practice starts with a goal kick and the players take their starting positions. The red team "press high" with 2 strikers looking to mark the centre backs and 2 wingers pressing the full backs. To allow the blue players to see the bigger picture and achieve reasonable success, we only have 1 opposing midfield player (3 v 1 overload in the centre).

Depending on the age or level of the players, you can instruct the 5 red players to "press passively" without tackling at first until progress is shown. Once the understanding improves, you can progress to a fully competitive game.

Coaching Points

1. Can the keeper, full back or centre back trigger the movement pattern by calling out "Cut"?
2. Can the centre back make a diagonal forward run across and in front of the pressing opponent (decoy run)?
3. Can the full back "drop down the line" looking to receive a pass (side-on) from the keeper?
4. If the red striker fails to track the inside run of the centre back, and there is space to play into, can the keeper play a weighted pass into space for the centre back to run onto? If so, can the centre back move forward with the ball?
5. Alternatively, if the red striker tracks the centre back's diagonal forward run, can the keeper "ping" a pass out wide to the arriving full back as he drops down the line (as shown in the diagram)?
6. Can you use good disguise to conceal your intentions?
7. Can you time and coordinate your movements effectively to lose markers?
8. Can you use a good open body position to play diagonal forward passes through the opponent pressure?

'The Cut' Variation: The Centre Back Makes a Forward Run to Receive from the Goalkeeper

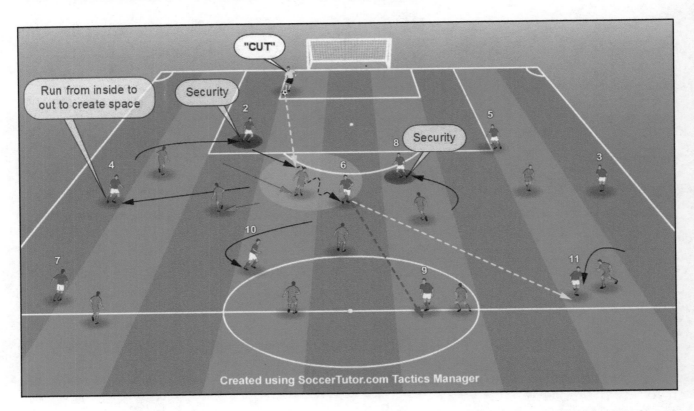

The diagram shows another example of 'The Cut' combined with a variation of 3 players rotating positions. This time it is a midfielder, a full back and a centre back (4, 2 and 6 in the diagram).

Here the centre back (6) tucks in, preparing early as the keeper looks up to play.

- Can the centre back (6) now run across his marker, open up and signal for the ball?

- If the centre back gets in front of his marker and creates space to run into, can the keeper play a well weighted pass into his path?

- If yes, can the centre back run forward with the ball, looking to deliver a diagonal forward pass? This might be a ground ball pass into the channels for No.11, 9 or 10 to run onto.

- If those passing options are blocked, can the centre back deliver a lofted pass in behind the defensive line for the on-running forwards?

- For this coordinated movement to work, can the nearest midfielder (4 or 8) cut across to open up the space for the centre back's forward run with the ball? If so, this midfielder (4) will end up in a wide position. In other words, he has effectively rotated positions with the full back (2) who should respond by tucking inside and into the centre back position to provide "security". Meanwhile, the centre back has driven forward with the ball into the midfield role.

As you can see in the diagram, these three movements equal a rotation of 3. This time, instead of the rotation taking place between the 3 central midfielders, it has taken place on the flank and involved the centre back (6), the full back (2) and a midfielder (4).

Again, it is important to note that the same rotation be explored on BOTH flanks in order for all players to understand the movement and to see the bigger picture.

PLAYING OUT FROM THE BACK BY SWITCHING PLAY / CHANGING POINT OF ATTACK

The examples in the next section show how to combine 'The Cut' with the rotation of 3 central midfielders, plus a quick switch of play (recycling through the keeper).

This can open up exciting opportunities to attack. The quicker and more precisely it's done, the better, as the opponents will likely be "pushed up high", hoping their pressure will secure a turnover in our defensive third. This high line of opponent pressure, where it can be broken and gaps found to play through, presents a well organised and possession based team with lots of opportunities to carve open exciting attacking channels and scoring opportunities. What follows are 3 effective examples of recycling through the keeper, each one starting with 'The Cut'.

THE ROLE OF THE KEEPER WHEN BUILDING UP PLAY

The Key Role of the Goalkeeper When 'The Cut' is Closed Down

As part of coaching the patterns of play outlined in this book, you will need to do a fair degree of one-to-one work with your keeper. Perhaps you can arrange for him to come early to training where you can use the tactics board and a bit of practical training to coach the basic movements and passing options. Your keeper can then go on to explore these in the subsequent training session. Needless to say, you will also need to work with your keeper as much as possible to progress his ground-ball passing skills.

Keepers can often be weak in the range of passing skills needed. Hence, it is vital that you work with them including one-to-one, in order to enhance their composure on the ball and their technical ability to distribute with precision, especially along the floor and over varying distances. That is why we have devoted this section to the role of the keeper.

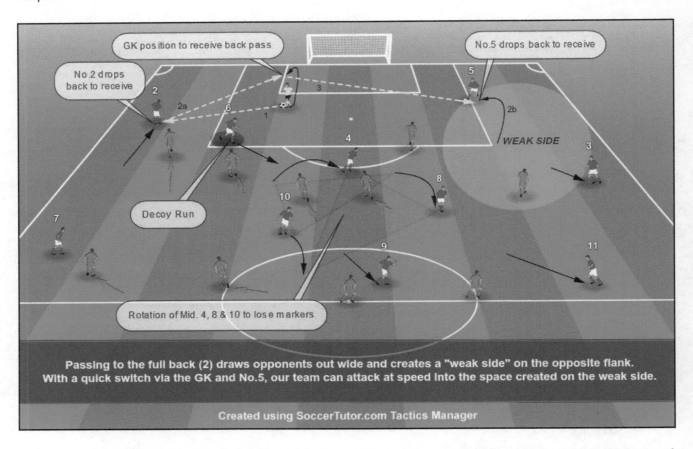

Passing to the full back (2) draws opponents out wide and creates a "weak side" on the opposite flank. With a quick switch via the GK and No.5, our team can attack at speed into the space created on the weak side.

Created using SoccerTutor.com Tactics Manager

In this example, the right back (2) is under pressure and passes back to the keeper.

- Can the keeper look to "open up" with a positive first touch, aiming to switch the ball to the opposite flank?

- Meanwhile, can the centre back on the opposite side (5) look to drop back along the side of the box? If so, is he "side-on" and looking to provide an outlet for the keeper's pass?

Assuming that the centre back's movement is not tracked by an opponent, the keeper can now "recycle" or "switch" the play to the less populated flank. *If this passing*

sequence is executed with precision and speed, all sorts of spaces and opportunities open up to play out and attack quickly. Here's a way to put it to the players:

What appears as a retreat, a failed attempt to play out from the right flank, works more like a decoy. It acts as a means to lure opponents away to achieve an intended goal. In this example the goal is a rapid attack down the opposite, unattended flank!

So, the more you allow your opponents to assume you're "cornered" or, at best, just hoping to "play it safe" with a lateral (sideways) pass, the better.

- Then with pace and precision, can your players seize their chance?

- *Can they quickly switch the play and change the point of attack, exploiting the open space to play quickly into the strikers with good support arriving?*

- If so, as in the diagram above, it'll be your opponents in desperate straits, compacted on the opposite flank, all out of balance, and struggling to recover. Can your team now finish off with an attempt on goal?

The diagram example shows the position (to the side of the goal) where the keeper should move to after passing to the full back (2). This allows the keeper to provide a good and safe supporting angle behind the ball in case the full back is closed down by an opponent and needs an outlet to "set" the ball back to.

By positioning himself wide of the goal post, the keeper is in a safer area to receive a back pass. If the keeper miss-controls this back pass and/or has an opponent rush in to press him, he still remains in a relatively safe space to quickly amend for any errors or, if necessary, look to clear the ball with a lofted pass out wide, for example, into the winger (e.g. No. 7).

Playing Out from the Back by Switching Play

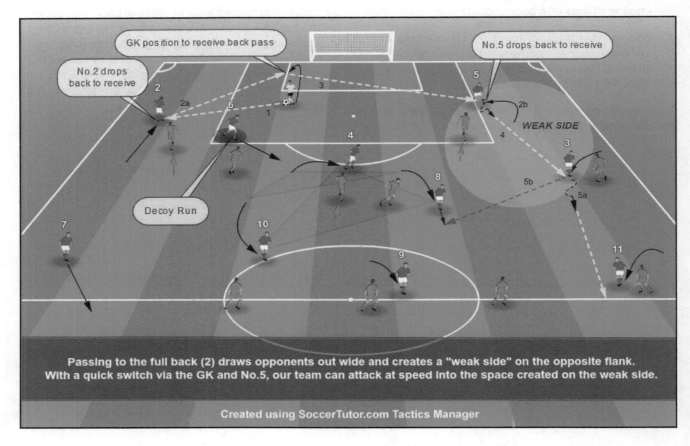

Passing to the full back (2) draws opponents out wide and creates a "weak side" on the opposite flank. With a quick switch via the GK and No.5, our team can attack at speed into the space created on the weak side.

Created using SoccerTutor.com Tactics Manager

So here we progress the same scenario that begins with the team attempting The Cut. However, due to intensive opponent pressure, the ball goes back to the keeper who looks to quickly recycle the play across to the opposite wing.

To assist the keeper in this, the opposite side centre-back (No.5) drops down the 18 yard line in order to create space to receive a pass. If this is done well and done quickly, the No.5 should have the time to control the ball with the option to play into the inside run of the left back (No.3 in diagram), who should be quick to get out wide so he can play his part. No.3 can then either run with the ball, looking to advance with pace and open up possibilities or, otherwise, can he play a quick forward pass into one of the strikers?

Alternatively, assuming these more direct (vertical) passing options are blocked, the No.5 can "bounce" the ball (first time pass) off the rotating midfielder No.4 and into the left back. The left back also has the No.8 making a supporting run.

In all, there should be plenty of options to play forward into the striker or into the inside run of the winger (No.11) etc. The quicker this is done the better.

Meanwhile, with opponents out of balance and scrambling to recover defensive positions, can your team take advantage and finish with an attempt on goal?

To some extent, this whole scenario needs to be handled as if it were a quick counter-attack, even though the trigger was through setting up a decoy rather than from achieving a "turn-over" of possession.

And to maximise your chances of success, can your 3 attackers and the No.10 show good acceleration to assist with forward runs looking to receive down the channels or in the space behind your opponent back-line? We will cover more on this in the Incision and Finish Phases to follow.

Continued... What if the Centre Back is Marked?

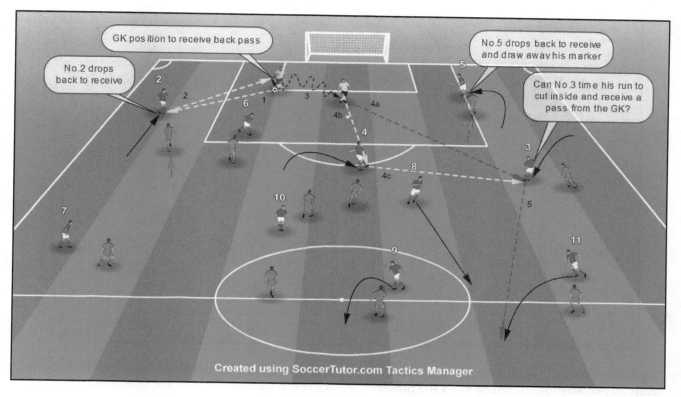

In this variation, the centre-back (5) drops back down the 18 yard line and is closed down by the striker.

- **_In this situation, can the full back (3) cut inside into the channel that opens up? (As shown above)_**

- Can the full back (3) get in front of his marker and become the outlet for a diagonal cross field pass from the keeper?

Obviously, this pass will only work when the channel has clearly opened up and there is space to play a weighted pass. As we have seen, this requires the keeper to play out quickly, while our opponents remain compact on the opposite flank.

If the channel hasn't opened up, sometimes the keeper will have space to run with the ball across his box (as shown in the diagram), and a gap then opens up or the opponents switch off, at which point the same move can be attempted successfully.

If neither of these options is available, the keeper can play a lofted long pass towards the opposite winger (11). Alternatively, he can pass to the deepest midfielder in the centre (4) who, if pressed, can "bounce" the ball (first time pass) wide to the full back No.3 (see the yellow arrows in the diagram). For a more attacking option, the keeper could also look to ping a forward pass into the

forward run of the No.8, opening up a number of exciting attacking possibilities as previously discussed.

The key to success is to adapt quickly using the basic movement patterns outlined. Players will then uncover other ways out and emerge with the ball in space, looking to mount a quick attack with good support arriving.

The last 2 sections have shown how 'The Cut' can work in a number of different and effective ways:

1. *The centre back can run diagonally across his marker, dragging him away to open up space for the full back to drop down the line and receive.*

2. *Using another version of the same basic move, the centre back can drop back down the 18 yard line to receive and create space for the full back to cut inside and receive in space, looking to play forward.*

3. *We've seen how these variations of 'The Cut' can be used to good effect in isolation. We've also seen how you can combine them both to set a trap or a decoy to draw your opponents over to one flank, thus opening up the opposite "weaker" side to attack at speed.*

The Goalkeeper's Support Position When Switching Play

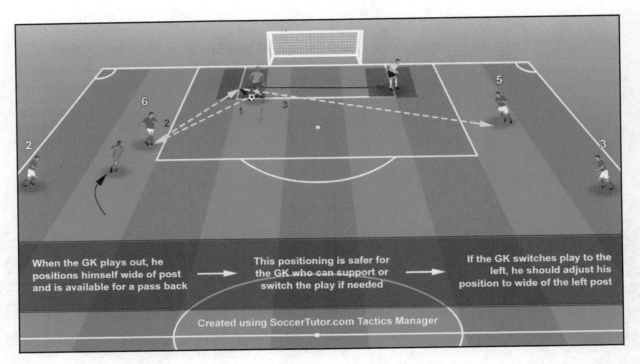

| When the GK plays out, he positions himself wide of post and is available for a pass back | This positioning is safer for the GK who can support or switch the play if needed | If the GK switches play to the left, he should adjust his position to wide of the left post |

Created using SoccerTutor.com Tactics Manager

This diagram shows where the keeper should look to adjust his positioning once he's received and passed across to the centre back on the opposite side (No.5). The "safe areas" for the keeper are represented by the highlighted red areas either side of the goal posts. The keeper's movement is indicated by the black arrows.

- Can the keeper quickly adjust his position after delivering a pass?

- Can he provide good support behind the ball to receive a pass back in case the centre back (5) is closed down by an opponent?

- If the keeper is closed down, can he keep his cool and play out to the No.5 or No.3 where they have space to advance?

The key to success is for the keeper and supporting players to always work hard to keep these numerous passing options open.

- Can the players work hard and show good awareness to create these patterns in competitive games?

- Can players retain good composure under pressure?

- When exploring these approaches to "playing out", can your players show good ability on the ball, good anticipation and coordination in their movements?

The exercises and games in this book are designed to encourage all these aspects, so they are game-related and specifically targeted to help players develop these necessary skills and awareness. The rest is up to you and

your players in terms of how intelligent/dedicated you can be in applying these tactics, turning them into reality.

For both the coach and the players it is important to encourage **PATIENCE** and a **COOL HEAD** at all times. This applies not just when the team are in possession, but also when mistakes are made and the ball is lost. At such times, *patience and a positive mind-set is vital to success, especially in the early "skills acquisition phase". Players must be given the time and space to learn these tactics individually and as a team.*

In many ways, this is the hardest aspect for both coach and player to adjust to. You will need to allow for the inevitable mistakes in competitive games (some costly in terms of possible goals conceded), but rather than view these mistakes as negative, you should see them as an important part of the learning process. I would urge you to always remain patient and positive with your players. Try to focus on where you can assist them technically and tactically. Try to design and adapt your practices so players can see for themselves the many options this style of play opens up.

As well as defining the bigger picture, you will need to work one-to-one with players to help correct mistakes and focus their attention on areas that require improvement. This is, of course, what makes for a good technical coach. It also offers you and your players the best chance to take your skills and your game intelligence to the next level.

Goalkeeper Support Angles & Accurate Passing to Switch Play

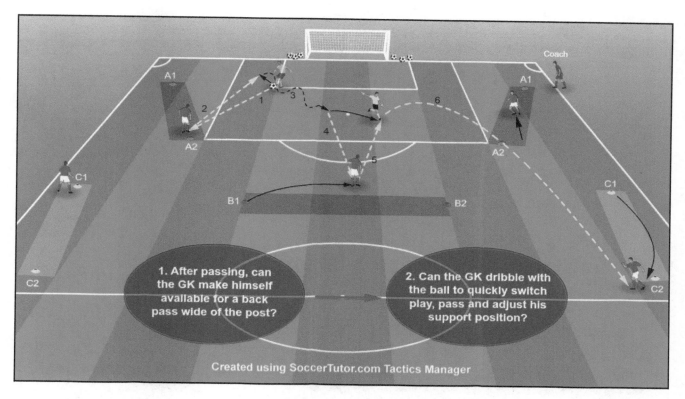

Practice Organisation

Using half a full sized pitch, the goalkeeper practices passing to various positions on the pitch and then moving into a supporting position to receive a pass back.

Challenge 1: Can the keeper play a crisp sequence of ground passes into the key target players? Can these players offer a passing outlet to the keeper by rotating between the cones? In the diagram above, A1 is where the full backs might look to receive a pass when they "drop down the line" (as part of 'The Cut'). A2 is the start position for the centre backs at goal kicks. B1 and B2 are start positions for two of our rotating midfielders. C1 is the typical start position at goal kicks for the full backs and C2 for the wingers.

Challenge 2: On receiving the ball, can the players "ping" the ball back to the keeper? Can the keeper then "open up" with his first touch, looking to play across to the opposite side or into the midfielder?

The keeper practices his short/medium ground and long passing skills. Can he deliver passes into all the key positions and quickly assume a good support position to receive a back pass? This practice can be incorporated into the keeper's pre-match warm up with the roles of the players taken by coaches and the substitute keeper.

Progression: Add a player to apply pressure on the keeper once the ball is passed back. The keeper must take a positive first touch away from oncoming pressure and look to recycle the ball to the opposite side or play it long.

Coaching Points

1. Can the keeper ensure support players are prepared to receive a pass before he looks to play?
2. Can the centre backs and full backs drop down the line, looking to receive the pass side-on from the keeper?
3. Can the keeper take a positive first touch away from opponent pressure and switch play to the opposite side? Can he do this with 2 touches (control and pass)?
4. Alternatively, if the keeper has no or minimal pressure, can he quickly change direction, running with the ball, before "pinging" a pass out to the centre back or full back (dropping back) on the opposite side?
5. Can the keeper use communication when necessary to assist teammates as they look to provide good support?

Switching Play Through the Goalkeeper Using 'The Cut' & 'The Switch' (Game Specific Practice)

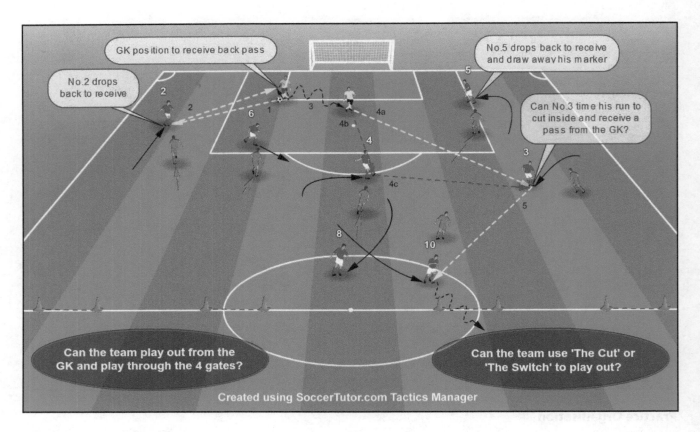

Practice Organisation

Using half a full sized pitch we mark out 4 cone gates (3 yards wide) on the halfway line. The blue team have a keeper, a back four (2, 5, 6 & 3) and 3 midfielders (4, 8 & 10) - you can use cones to mark their starting positions. The red team act as high pressing opponents with 2 forwards, 2 wingers and 2 central midfielders.

- Can the team "play out" from the keeper? Can they look to play and dribble through a cone gate?
- Can the keeper combine with his back 4 using 'The Cut' and 'The Switch'? ('The Switch' is shown in the diagram)
- Can the team explore these coordinated movements on both flanks against "high-pressing" opponents?
- Can the players assume their start positions quickly as the keeper prepares to take a goal kick?
- Can the 2 red strikers start central, then look to press the centre backs?
- Can the 2 red wingers press the full backs?
- Can the 2 red midfielders look to press our central midfielders as they rotate and look to receive?

Start the practice with "passive" pressing. Once the players achieve success playing out, then change to full pressure. Make sure the opposition team (red) maintain "high pressure". There is also an option to use "man-marking".

Coaching Points

1. Can the keeper ensure supporting players are prepared to receive a pass as he looks up ready to play?
2. Can the centre backs and full backs explore 'The Cut' and receive passes "side-on" to the keeper?
3. If receiving a back pass, can the keeper take a positive first touch "away from opponent pressure"? If so, can he switch play to the opposite wing? Can he do this with 2 touches (control and pass preferably on the ground)?
4. If the keeper is not under pressure, can he quickly change direction with the ball before "pinging" a pass out to the other centre back or out to the opposite full back as he drops down the line or moves inside to receive?
5. Can the keeper communicate well to assist teammates in providing good support movements to play out?

    Coaching Combination Play

When to "Go Long" to Break Through the Opposition's High Pressing

There will be moments in competitive games where the best option for your keeper will be to "go long". You will need to coach your keeper good long-ball kicking technique so he can execute these passes precisely. You will also want to work with him on who amongst his teammates is best placed to receive such a pass. Most importantly, to control possession, you will need to ensure your keeper understands when it is appropriate to use the long ball pass.

Coaches committed to possession football need to guard against their keeper simply launching long balls up field. The odds in such moments are, at best 50-50. And, of course 50-50 means it's likely to result in uncertain outcomes. Teams coached to dominate possession avoid 50-50 scenarios as much as possible. The long ball should involve a coordinated reaction from the players.

The diagram shows our team taking a goal kick. In this scenario, our opponents know we like to play out from the back. They have begun to press with increasing intensity, hoping to recover possession in or around our box. They are hoping for a quick turnover and, if possible, a deadly attempt on goal! Typically they will push 2 or more attackers "up high" and when our keeper plays the ball, they will look to press "man-for-man".

In the diagram example, our team try 'The Cut' but our opponents are now "savvy to it". They are wary of the decoy runs and instead press hard on whoever has the ball, including our keeper whenever he receives. They also work hard to cut off options including the pass to the opposite flank.

In situations like this, it makes sense for your keeper to target a precise long pass (clearance) out to the nearest winger. Can the winger (7 or 11) anticipate this and adjust his position as the keeper "shapes to go long"? Can they move into space on the wing e.g. between the opposition's full back and winger? Can this player adopt a good open body position so he can see the field of play and the keeper executing the kick?

Advanced teammates need to be quick to run into supporting positions so that when the ball lands, your team have a numerical advantage around the ball.

The principal benefits of the long pass in these situations:

- A lofted pass could eliminate numerous opponents as they are likely pressing "up high" and will not expect this counter move. Chances are your team can mount a quick attack leading to an attempt on goal!

- It will undermine your opponents "high press" tactics. Chances are they will soon decide it is safer to "drop off", leaving your team more space and time to play out from the back once again.

CHAPTER 2
THE INCISION PHASE

* For the examples in this chapter we have used the 4-3-3 formation, but you can adapt all the movement patterns and practices to suit the formation of your team.

THE INCISION PHASE

So far, we have looked at the build up phase and the consolidation phases in possession play. We've presented a number of coordinated movement patterns your team can explore to play out from the keeper and advance with good possession into the opponent's half. Now we start to look at the incision phase. This is where the team in possession look to get beyond the defensive lines of their opponents with penetrating passes supported by good movement, aiming to score a goal. It's that simple. Or not!

With so many possibilities available when it comes to attacking football and depending on the tactics, team formation, game management etc, the examples to follow are strictly built on the foundations already set out in the build up and consolidation phases. In other words, the incision phase starts where the consolidation phase ends. And here the quality coach will focus on encouraging his team to maintain possession through clearly defined and coordinated movements.

The coach will need to work with units of players to ensure they become clearly aware of the key triggers to progress the play. Initially this will likely involve the coach using a fair degree of "command style" coaching. However, the purpose of this is simply to get all your players "on the same page" with regard to how they might coordinate their on and off-ball movements.

Once the players have learned the "tools" and once they see how effective these tools can be, then as the coach you can step back and let them take centre stage. You will, of course, still be there to assist but it will be more about tweaking with good, concise technical and tactical information plus, of course, lots of positive encouragement. Chances are you will soon find your team progressing on the patterns of play you have covered together. The ingenuity and creativity of your players when put under pressure will bring out all manner of exciting variations in play. You will also have the satisfaction of watching them use their own unique individual strengths to build on the key collective triggers and patterns you have invited them to explore. The players are the actors. They bring the game plan to life on the field of play. What a good coach does is provide the spark and set the stage for this collective action. Hence, the wider and deeper your understanding and imagination as the coach, the more scope you can give your players to express themselves and turn effective ideas into exciting reality.

To start off I want to explain the basic building block concept that will help you maintain a clear vision of the effective shape your players should adopt as they pass and move their way "through the thirds", aiming to create scoring opportunities. I will then outline some very effective exercises you can use with your players to reinforce their understanding of these basic building blocks. These can be used as warm-ups to kick start your sessions.

We have seen how important patience is in maintaining possession, but this patience is worthless if players lack awareness and a "killer instinct". The best way of honing this is through exercises that combine maintaining possession with coordinated movements to create space to play forward. So, after looking at the basic fundamentals behind strong incision play, we will progress and look at how best to "switch play" from flank to flank, and examine why it is so vital. Quite simply, the better your team get at doing this, the more likely they will go on to dominate possession. However, the whole purpose of doing this, as we shall see, is to open up gaps through which we can advance the play, with the aim of creating opportunities to score.

In the build-up and consolidation phases, we looked at the vital role played by the rotating midfield 3. As we progress up the pitch and into the incision phase, we can see how variations of the same movement patterns can be explored as an effective means to play through pressure. Again, this is another very good reason why it is so important to get your players proficient at playing out from the keeper and through the thirds. What they learn in the build-up phases can to some extent be reapplied in varied forms in the incision phase of attacking play.

We will then go on to look at a number of very useful attacking patterns of play with key practices you can coach to help your team create scoring opportunities. I have given these patterns of play simple names to aid learning such as 'The Classic', 'The X', 'The Cut' (incision phase), 'The Open Gate' etc.

We will also look at counter attacking in this section and suggest a few effective practices to explore.

Playing Through Compact & Well Balanced Opponents

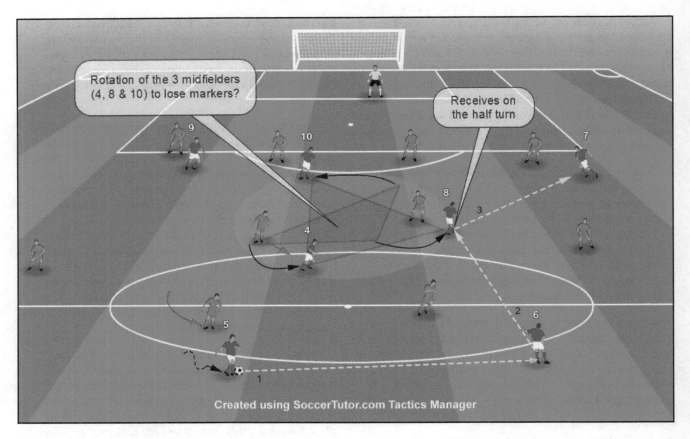

The above scenario is a good place to begin exploring the incision phase of play. In the diagram, we see the opposition are relatively compact and well organised in central areas. For the attacking team, the challenge is to find ways to break through their defensive lines. So what options for combination play can we explore?

In this example, our team aim to switch the play (across the pitch) with the key purpose of searching for gaps to play through.

- Can the midfielders adopt an effective *off-set triangle* shape as shown?

- Can they then look to *rotate positions,* adapting what they've learned in the build-up phase?

The aim, once again, is to lose tight opposition markers and create space to receive and attack. As the ball travels between the centre backs, our midfielders rotate and arrive in space. No.8 receives a pass from the centre back (6) on the half turn. The pass itself eliminates 3 or 4 opponents and No.8 now has many promising options. I have outlined the following 3:

1. Turn and dribble forward with the ball, looking to draw defenders towards him and combine with the No.10 and No.7.

2. "Bounce" the ball (pass first time) to No.7 as shown in the diagram. If the full back hasn't pushed up, the No.8 could then make an overlapping run into the wide channel, looking for a return (reverse) pass.

3. With the No.7 tucking in, the No.8 also has the option of playing the ball wide to an overlapping full back if they have made a run forward to receive.

Switching Play Using Rotations in Advanced Areas: Losing Markers & Creating Gaps to Play Through

The opposition (reds) are sitting back, largely compact and balanced.

- What do you notice about the shape and movement of our back line (2, 3, 5 & 6) and our 3 midfielders (4, 8 and 10)?

As you can see, it is essentially a simple variation of the coordinated movement patterns the players have used when playing through pressure in the build-up phase (previous chapter). The 2 centre backs have split and this time two of the midfielders (8 & 10) have quickly formed a rotating triangle with the striker (9). As the ball travels across, the players' 3 way movement creates space as they lose their markers, looking to receive a forward pass on the half turn (see No.8 in the diagram).

I would recommend using a tactics board to demonstrate each step and discuss the rotations with your players. It is much easier for them to see the shape when it is set out this way. You might add, "it's just like it is when we rotate to lose markers in our own half" e.g. when playing through pressure from the keeper.

All the hard work they have done on improving their movements in the build-up phase will now help them play through opponent pressure. *They can use variations of the same basic shape and movement patterns in the previous phases to play through pressure in the opposition's half.*

Having advanced this far up the pitch, the team are now just one step from the finishing phase. Adopting a strong attacking shape and recognising the importance of good mobility in central and wide areas, the players should soon grow in confidence, exploring ways to break through even the more organised defensive lines.

Obviously in real game situations there will be plenty of occasions where only 1 or 2 players will make these movements to lose markers. Otherwise, it would itself become predictable and opponents would adapt. The point is that rotating along these lines adds vital mobility to assist your team to lose markers and play through central areas. If these movements are well timed, even just one of them, there may well be the opportunity to play forward and help create scoring opportunities. This should be reason enough to use these rotations in advanced central areas with your team.

Continued... Switching Play Using Rotations in Advanced Areas

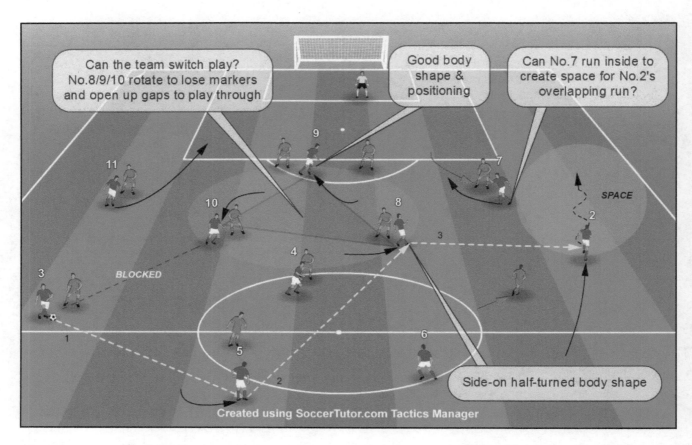

Can the team switch play? No.8/9/10 rotate to lose markers and open up gaps to play through

Good body shape & positioning

Can No.7 run inside to create space for No.2's overlapping run?

SPACE

BLOCKED

Side-on half-turned body shape

Created using SoccerTutor.com Tactics Manager

In more advanced central areas the player rotations will involve a likely combination of midfielders and attackers. In this situation, 3 players rotate (8, 9 and 10) as the play evolves.

Firstly, the No.10 drops back looking to support the left back (3) on the ball, however the option is closed down. Instead, No.3 passes back to the centre back (5) who plays into the path of No.8 who has timed his arrival (rotation) to receive a diagonal pass (note his body position on receiving the ball should be side-on/half turned). With close pressure on No.8, he spreads the ball wide into the run of the advancing full back who has started his run into space early.

The striker (9) takes his cue from these movements. As shown in the diagram, he drifts in the opposite direction to the traveling ball and the opposition's back line who are "shifting across" to press and cover. This is good movement from the No.9 and makes him difficult to pick up. This is because defenders must decide who will take responsibility for him. This is not easy as they are moving in the opposite direction! It will get even trickier for them if the No.9 maintains an open body position, side-on, facing the ball and looking to get in between defenders.

- Better still, can the striker get on the "blind side" of the centre backs ("on the shoulder"), looking to make a run inside to finish from an incoming pass or cross?

If the pass or cross doesn't arrive, the No.9 and No.10 can look to rotate once again, aiming to lose markers etc (there will be more on this in the finishing phase chapter to follow).

These are all good coaching points you can explore with your striker, building on the basic rotations we have been looking at.

Overall the high degree of mobility will make it hard to defend against, especially if the attackers work tirelessly to find little pockets of space between the opposition's midfield and defensive lines.

Switching Play to Create Scoring Opportunities Using "Inverted Wingers" in a Dynamic SSG

Practice Organisation

Using half a full sized pitch we have an 8 v 7 (+GK) situation - you can adapt the player numbers according to availability. We mark out 3 red cone gates on the halfway line (3 yards wide) and 5 blue cones in the positions shown.

The blue attacking team have 2 full backs (2 & 3), a defensive midfielder (4), 2 attacking midfielders (8 & 10), 2 wingers (7 & 11) and a striker (9). The red defending team have a back 4 who defend near the edge of the penalty area, 2 defensive midfielders and 1 attacking midfielder. Limit the players to 1 or 2 touches.

The practice begins with a full back passing to the defensive midfielder (4). This is a trigger for central rotations and the forward run of the full back (as shown in the diagram). The blue team aim to create chances and score. If the reds win possession, they have 6 seconds to counter attack and dribble through any of the 3 cone gates.

Practice Conditions

1. The team must start by switching the play as a trigger for rotations from the central players (8, 9, 10).
2. The team must play through at least one central attacking player (8, 9 or 10) before they can attack the goal.
3. Only one full back (2 or 3) can move forward at a time.

Coaching Points

1. Can the team provide good shape and support angles to allow them to switch the play quickly from flank to flank?
2. As they switch play, can the central players rotate positions to lose markers, looking to find space or gaps in the opposition's defence to play through?
3. Can they deliver their passes with "ping" to take advantage of any space created through which they can attack (e.g. into the opposite winger)?
4. Can advanced attackers make 2 movements (check away before moving to receive)? Good timing is vital.
5. Can the striker move in the opposite direction to that of the ball, trying to get on the blind side of the defenders?
6. Can the players make effective, well-timed runs into the box to finish off scoring opportunities?

Switching Play to Create Goal Chances in a 7 v 7 (+2) Small Sided Game

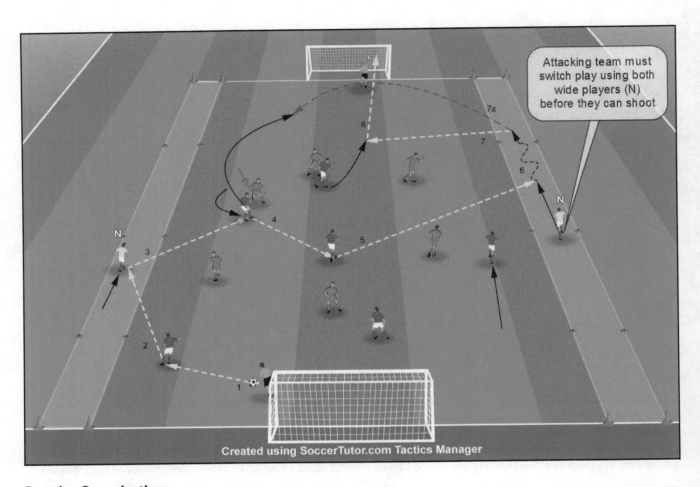

Attacking team must switch play using both wide players (N) before they can shoot

Created using SoccerTutor.com Tactics Manager

Practice Organisation

In a 40 x 60 yard area, we play a 7 v 7 small sided game with 2 extra neutral players who are limited to 3 touches and are not allowed to leave the marked out side zones.

Teams can set up in a 3-2-1 or 2-2-2 formation. The practice begins with either keeper.

The aim for both teams is to switch play from one side zone (flank) to the other. Both neutral players must touch the ball before a team is allowed to shoot at goal. If the defending team win possession (reds in diagram), they have the same aims and restrictions, so must play via both wide neutral players prior to attempting to score.

Coaching Points

1. Manage the defending team to make sure they defend in an organised way, maintaining pressure, cover and balance as a compact unit.

2. Can teams try to build play "through the thirds"?

3. Ensure both keepers are fully involved in helping the teams switch the play.

Progression

The wide neutral player on the opposite side can leave their zone to attack the far post and try to score.

Forwards Using Width to Create Space to Attack in the Centre in a 7 v 7 Small Sided Game

Practice Organisation

We split a 40 x 50 yard area into thirds and mark out 2 side channels (8-10 yards wide which are only for use in the attacking third). We play a 7 v 7 small sided game but you can adapt the numbers depending on player availability.

Both teams use a 2-2-2 formation with 2 players in each third. Can the teams "play through the thirds" from defence, through midfield and into the attacking zone? Once the ball is played into the attacking zone, one midfielder can enter to create a 3 v 2 overload.

If the defending team win possession, they attack with the same conditions. The practice begins when the coach plays the ball in. There are no corners or throw-ins. If the ball goes out, resume with the opposite keeper.

- *Can the 2 forwards always look to "push high and wide" when their team attack?*
- Can a midfielder support the 2 forwards to create a 3 v 2 attacking advantage in the final third?

Coaching Points

1. Can the attackers quickly adjust their positions to provide width in the attacking third?
2. Can an attacking midfielder look to exploit space created by the wide movement of the 2 strikers and attack?
3. Can midfielders and attackers combine quickly to play through any space created in central areas?
4. Can attackers lose their markers and receive a pass? If so, can they turn and attack looking to win their 1 v 1? If not, can they pass back into the path of a supporting midfielder?
5. If midfielders switch play, can they show awareness of movements of strikers? They should look to play into them when possible and quickly support the pass.

VARIATION
Forwards "Tucking in" to Create Space to Attack Out Wide in a 7 v 7 Small Sided Game

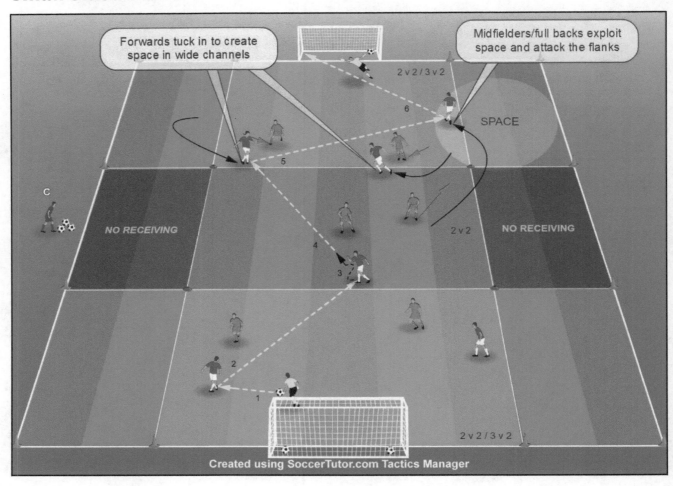

Practice Organisation

The set up of this practice is identical to the previous practice, but we now focus on the following:

- Key Purpose of the Practice: *Can the 2 attackers always look to "tuck in" when their team attack?*
- *Can a midfielder support the 2 attackers by making an overlapping run to create a 3 v 2 attacking advantage in the final third?*
- Can the defending team demonstrate good positioning/shape, recover possession and attack the opposite goal?

Coaching Points

1. Can the attackers quickly adjust their positions and "tuck in" in the attacking third (e.g. keep the 2 flanks clear)?
2. Can an attacking midfielder look to exploit any space created in wide areas, looking to make an overlapping or inside run to attack on goal?
3. Can midfielders and attackers combine quickly to take advantage of these runs and finish?
4. Can attackers lose their markers and receive a pass? If so, can they turn`and attack looking to win their 1 v 1? If not, can they pass back into the path of a supporting midfielder?
5. Can midfielders switch play while showing good awareness of the movements of the forwards?
6. Can the midfielders look to play into the forwards when possible and start their overlapping runs in good time to create good third-man running opportunities?
7. Can players use 1 or 2 touches when combining or show a positive attitude when turning to isolate a defender?
8. Can players make effective, well-timed attacking runs to finish off scoring opportunities?

COMBINATIONS IN WIDE AREAS

'The Classic I' Combination

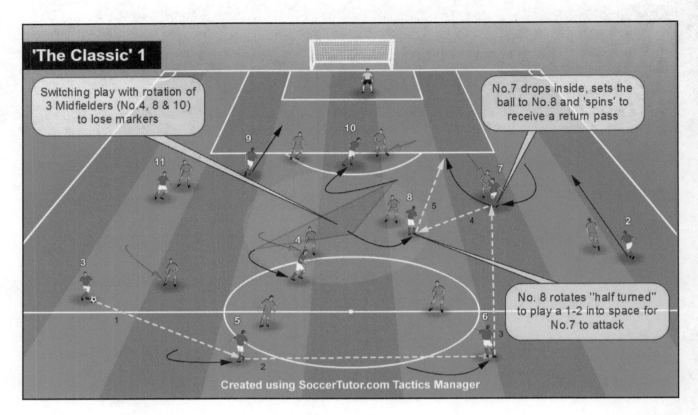

'The Classic' 1

Switching play with rotation of 3 Midfielders (No.4, 8 & 10) to lose markers

No.7 drops inside, sets the ball to No.8 and 'spins' to receive a return pass

No. 8 rotates "half turned" to play a 1-2 into space for No.7 to attack

Created using SoccerTutor.com Tactics Manager

The patterns of play illustrated above with high mobility shown in advanced central areas, provide a basic foundation for a whole range of attacking combinations.

Here I'm going to consider 3 tried and trusted options. Working with my players, I call these options the Classic 1, Classic 2 and Classic 3.

'The Classic 1' - for success it is vital that:

1. Players understand the coordinated movements and anticipate them to ensure they remain one step ahead of their opponents.

2. Players recycle/switch the ball quickly from one flank to the other, with all of the players always looking to play into rotating midfielders when and where gaps open up.

3. The wide players on the weak side (opposite flank) e.g. No.2 and No.7 in diagram, anticipate the switch of play and vary their responses in order to create space for themselves. For example, No.7 will need to decide whether to "stay high and wide", to "drop down the line" or "tuck in" looking to receive and turn or set a first time pass back.

4. When a player is tightly marked, it is essential he check away from his marker before moving to

receive a pass in space ("go-to-show"). In the diagram example, No.7 attempts this but the marker stays with him. This is why the No.7 looks to "bounce" the pass (play one-touch), setting the ball back and spinning to receive a quick return pass beyond his marker.

5. The full back (2) should take his cue for his movement from the positioning and movement of the right winger (7) in the following ways:

- If the right winger (7) moves out wide, can the right back (2) look to receive and "drive inside" with the ball?

- Alternatively, if the right winger (7) moves inside, can the right back (2) anticipate this and start an early and well-timed overlapping run? If so, he will likely provide a good support angle in the wide channel and help to create a possible "overload".

- If the full back receives high up the pitch, can he attack the goal, finish or attempt a cross/set back?

'The Classic 2' & 'The Classic 3' Combinations

In the examples shown here, the team recycle the play quickly while the attacking midfielders rotate, looking to create space and receive forward passes. Where gaps open up, and players have their heads up looking to play, this is the trigger to initiate coordinated patterns of play.

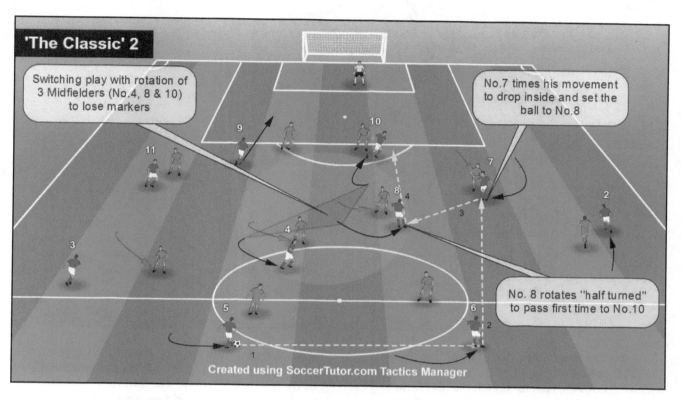

'The Classic' 2

Switching play with rotation of 3 Midfielders (No.4, 8 & 10) to lose markers

No.7 times his movement to drop inside and set the ball to No.8

No. 8 rotates "half turned" to pass first time to No.10

Created using SoccerTutor.com Tactics Manager

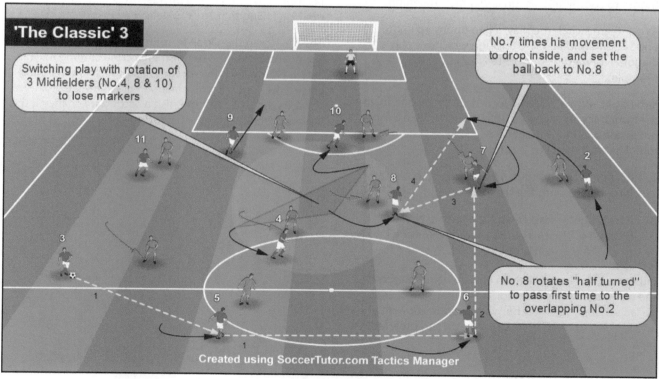

'The Classic' 3

Switching play with rotation of 3 Midfielders (No.4, 8 & 10) to lose markers

No.7 times his movement to drop inside, and set the ball back to No.8

No. 8 rotates "half turned" to pass first time to the overlapping No.2

Created using SoccerTutor.com Tactics Manager

'The Classic 3' Variation: The Winger Stays Wide

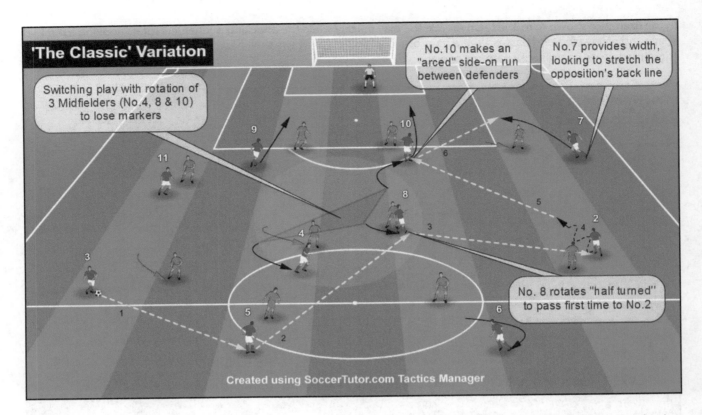

The scenario above shows a variation of 'The Classic 3'. The No.7 (or No.11 if played on the opposite wing) stays wide and "hugs the line" to "stretch the play", awaiting the trigger to coordinate his run and attack in behind.

As our team switch the play, a gap opens up in the opposition's midfield line through which we play a diagonal forward pass (No.5 to No.8 in our diagram example).

If the right winger (7) remains wide in this scenario, then the right back (2) can seize his chance to make a forward run inside and into the space available (an under-lapping run). The No.8 then has 2 options:

1. If he has space to turn, he can choose to play a forward pass into the No.10.

2. If he is tightly marked and the pass to No.10 is blocked off, he can instead set the ball wide into the path of the arriving right back (2).

Either way, the ball is likely to end up being played into the well-timed run of the No.10 ahead. This run needs to be "arced", aiming to get between 2 opposition defenders and looking to receive the ball side-on and preferably to feet.

The forward pass from the right back is the trigger for the right winger (7) to start his "blind side run" into the wide area, running inside so as to evade the opposing full back (as well as to avoid being offside). No.7 can now "go for goal" or, failing that, look to deliver a cross or cut-back.

The No.10 can then look to sprint into the box in line with the near post in time to finish off a cross coming in. The striker (9) meanwhile, can focus on getting on the blind side of the centre back, looking to finish from a cross towards the back post or finish a secondary chance if the keeper saves or spills the first attempt.

The Winger's Run Inside to Become the "Second Striker"

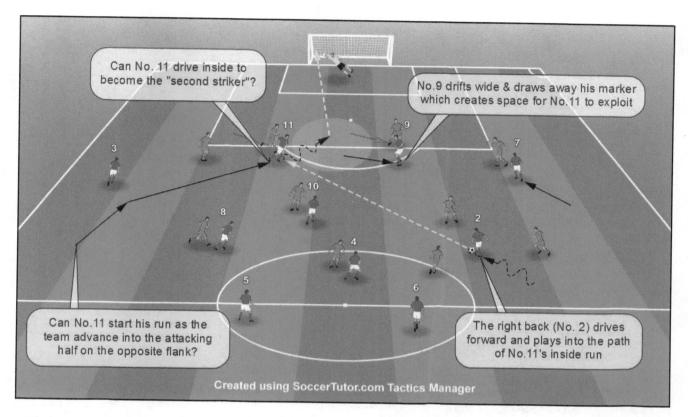

Can No. 11 drive inside to become the "second striker"?

No.9 drifts wide & draws away his marker which creates space for No.11 to exploit

Can No.11 start his run as the team advance into the attacking half on the opposite flank?

The right back (No. 2) drives forward and plays into the path of No.11's inside run

Created using SoccerTutor.com Tactics Manager

When playing a 4-3-3 or 4-2-3-1 formation, a very simple but effective tactic is to challenge the wingers to make forward runs to become the "second striker". This is widely used and works as follows:

- As the team progress play up one flank and cross the halfway line, can the winger on the opposite flank make a strong forward run into a more central attacking role?

This strong forward run gives your team "more bodies" in advanced areas and more potential for quick combination play to help create scoring opportunities.

If this forward and inside run of the winger is timed well, there is the potential for a long diagonal pass directly into his path (as shown in the diagram). Clever movement from the supporting striker (9) can help this happen by dragging away the centre back markers and opening up space in the centre to attack.

Depending on how "attack-minded" your overall tactics are, there is another advantage to this attacking run. It also opens up the wide area for an overlapping run by a supporting full back. This can give your team all sorts of additional attacking options. In the diagram example, as the No.11 cuts inside and receives the pass, it opens up the wide area for the left back (3) to attack. If his run is

well timed to beat the offside trap, the left back (3) could soon find himself in a 1 v 1 with the keeper. A simple combination would be for No.11 to pass to No.9 who plays a "killer" diagonal pass into the path of No.3's run in behind. He can then finish or cut the ball back for a teammate.

The possibilities are numerous. What happens and what doesn't happen will be down to your players and their powers of anticipation and creativity. However, by introducing a few clear guidelines, you the coach can help open up their horizons individually and as a team. This simple tactic should allow your players more freedom to express themselves in attack. It encourages quick combination play, looking to create scoring opportunities.

'The X' Combination

> No.11 drops to set the ball back to No.3 who 'pings' a pass into the arriving forward (No.10)

> Receiving on the half-turn, can No.10 take a touch and shoot, combine with No.11 or play into the overlapping run of No.3?

Created using SoccerTutor.com Tactics Manager

'The X' is another classic coordinated movement pattern you often see used by the better passing sides. It is something you may want to explore with your players. Again, let's look at this pattern of play based on the structured, yet highly mobile platform set in place in our build-up and consolidation phases. What distinguishes 'The X' is that it is an example of attacking flank play where the winger opts to stay wide e.g. looking at first to stretch the play, then drop down the line to receive. This is in contrast to the Classic 1, 2 and 3 combinations where we saw how the winger looks to tuck in or drop inwards.

The diagram shows the basic X pattern. It's an excellent means by which a team can go from the consolidation phase to the incision phase. *We call it 'The X' because it consists of 2 diagonal passes that cross in opposite directions* (No.5 into No.11 then No.3 into No. 9 or No. 10). Assuming good player anticipation, *'The X' can prove very effective, eliminating the opponents attacking and midfield lines with just 2 medium range diagonal passes.* When done well, this transition can take just 3 first time passes.

Variations might involve the full back receiving a set back pass from the winger and then dribbling the ball forward, before playing a "killer pass" into the arriving striker. It's power as an incisive movement can be seen in the way the second diagonal pass moves the ball into an advanced central area in front of the opposition's box.

- Receiving the ball on the half-turn, can the attacker (No.10 in diagram) take 1 touch and shoot?

- Alternatively, can he combine with the winger (e.g. No.11 in the diagram) who, assuming he has pressure behind, can "set and spin", looking to provide width and support to the receiving attacker.

- Otherwise, can the full back overlap to provide the width, assuming he has the pace to do it?

Alternatively, the diagram tells the story of a thousand words. It shows the centre back (5) playing a through pass into the left winger (11) who is tightly marked. The No.11 makes his "two movements" hoping to win space to turn

and receive. His marker, however, doesn't fall for it and remains "touch tight" so No.11 chooses to set a pass back to the left back (3).

For 'The X' to work, the left back (3) needs to have shown good anticipation and moved into a good supporting position "behind the ball". No.11 can now set a pass back to No.3 who pings a diagonal forward pass into No.9 or No.10 as this player arrives in space after a good double movement.

To succeed with this coordinated pattern of play, the players will need to develop a clear picture of how 'The X' movement works. To execute the pattern effectively, they will need to make good, well-timed movements to shake off markers, allowing 1 or 2 touch interplay. They then need to learn how to do this in variable conditions, including against opponents applying high pressure.

Using 'The X' in the transition from the incision phase to the finishing phase could involve the following:

1. Once No.11 has dropped down the line and set the ball back to the full back (3), he spins out around his marking opponent. The idea is for No.11 to quickly get into the wide channel. From here he can provide an excellent attacking support angle for the No.10 arriving into the central space to receive the final pass in 'The X' movement (see diagram). The No.10 can now play in the left winger (11) who can either drive inside and make a cut back pass or move out wide and whip in a cross.

2. Alternatively, the No.10 can combine with No.11, looking to isolate the opposition's full back and perhaps play a one-two around him to create a clear goal scoring chance.

3. The No.10 also has the option, if he receives in space, to open up and strike at goal from 25-30 yards. Failing that, when he arrives in space, he can look to turn and combine with the striker (9) before shooting.

'The X' can also be used when the team is playing out from a deeper position (i.e. in the build-up phase) e.g. with the centre back passing wide from the edge of his box. If the incisive pass from the full back is delivered with precision into a channel between the opposing full back and centre back (assuming they are pushed up around the halfway line), our No.9 or No.10 could easily find themselves "through on goal" in a foot race to the finishing phase.

Assuming our striker completes the move with a shot on goal, the team will have achieved a "long possession chain". This involves starting from the keeper and ending with an attempt on goal without the opposition touching the ball. Of course, this is the stuff of dreams, but get your team well drilled and aware and it can readily happen in any game. To my eye, this is when football becomes truly special as a spectacle and as a source of genuine, exciting entertainment. Teams with the ability to pull off extended patterns of play like this, retaining possession with strong momentum and quick interplay, set the gold standard in football!

On the following 2 pages we present 2 warm-up practices that are often used to explore the basic mechanics of 'The X'. You can then progress player understanding and awareness through the structured competitive practice we have presented. This will help players explore the 5 key incision combinations, as well as any variations they come up with themselves.

'The X' Passing Combination Warm Up

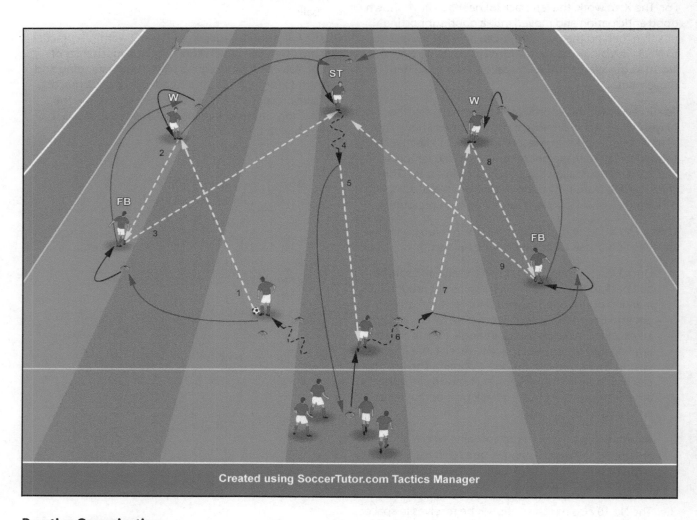

Created using SoccerTutor.com Tactics Manager

Practice Organisation

In a 40 x 40 yard area we have a minimum of 11 players and mark out 9 cones in the positions shown.

The practice starts on the left side with a diagonal forward pass towards the winger (W). The winger sets the ball back to the full back (FB) who plays another diagonal forward pass to the striker (ST). Once the striker receives the pass, he dribbles with the ball (at pace) and passes back to the starting gates.

The players rotate to the next position as shown (clockwise direction - blue arrows). We then repeat the same passing sequence to the right with players rotating positions in an anti-clockwise direction.

Ensure to position the cones so that every pass will need to be over 20 yards. This will help players improve their medium range ground passing skills.

Coaching Points

1. Use a tactics board to demonstrate the practice to ensure players understand the pass and move order.
2. Can you play a precise and driven pass along the ground to your teammate?
3. Can you make 2 movements, checking away before then moving to receive?
4. Can you successfully signal where you want the pass delivered?
5. Can you play using only *1 TOUCH*? (Maximum of 2 touches - receive and pass)

PROGRESSION
'The X' Passing Combination Warm Up with Pressure & Quick One-Two

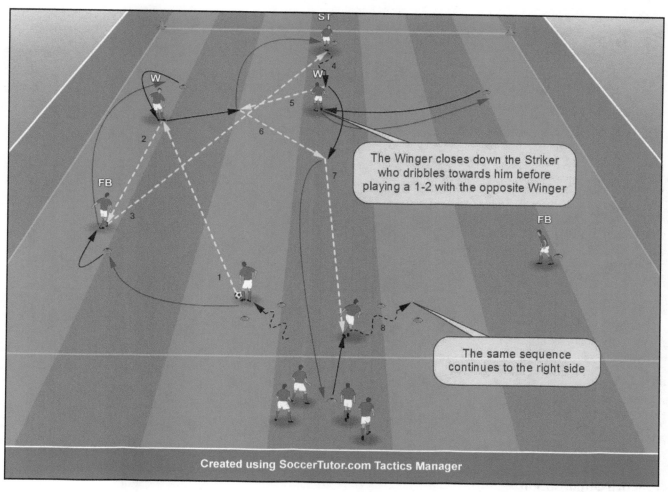

> The Winger closes down the Striker who dribbles towards him before playing a 1-2 with the opposite Winger

> The same sequence continues to the right side

Created using SoccerTutor.com Tactics Manager

Practice Organisation

Using the same structure and layout as the previous practice, we now have a passive opponent and an extra combination between the winger and striker after the third pass.

- As pass 3 is played into the striker, the winger on the opposite side runs across to close him down.
  Can the striker receive the pass and dribble the ball forward to engage his pressing opponent?
- As the opponent approaches, the winger moves inside and the striker plays a one-two with him. The advanced striker then passes back to the starting gates. The players all rotate positions in a clockwise direction as shown.

We then repeat the same sequence on the right with players rotating positions in an anti-clockwise direction. On the right, the pressing player (winger) comes in from the left.

The pressing players quickly return to their cone after the one-two is completed. Ensure to position the cones so that every pass will need to be over 20 yards. This will help players improve their medium range ground passing skills.

Coaching Points

1. Use the same coaching points as the previous practice.
2. The pressing player should only apply *PASSIVE PRESSURE* at first. Once the players are comfortable, you can progress this to more competitive *ACTIVE PRESSURE*.
3. Challenge the striker to dribble with the ball towards the pressing player and then play a well timed one-two with the supporting teammate. To be effective, the second pass must not be played too soon or too late!

Patterns of Play: Key Incision Phase Combinations (Opposed Practice)

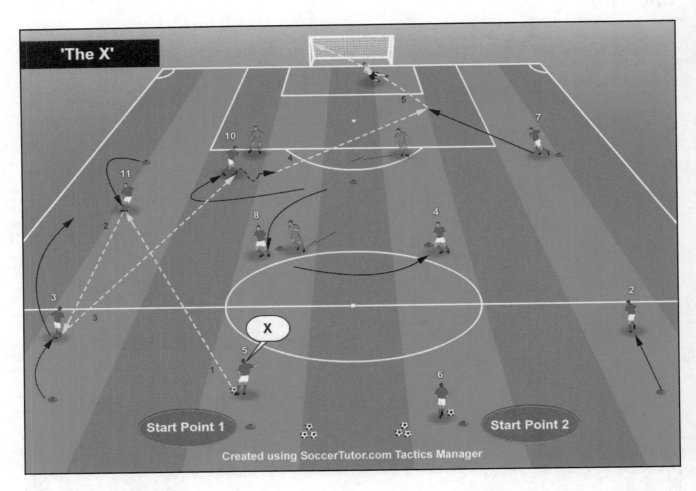

Practice Organisation

Using 3/4 of a full pitch we mark out 9 cones in the positions shown. We have a supply of balls at the start, in the 2 centre back positions (5 and 6). The blue team have a back 4, 3 rotating midfielders in the centre, 2 wingers and 1 striker. The red team have 2 centre backs on the edge of the penalty area and 1 midfielder in the centre (3 v 1 situation) who are all fully active.

The blue full backs and wingers are unopposed so limit them to 2 or 3 touches, depending on player age/ability. We alternate playing on the left and right, starting with one of the centre backs.

The aim for the blue players is to use one of the 5 key incision combinations we have learned in this section, to mount an attack on goal. The centre backs or the coach calls out the combination to be used (e.g. 'The X', 'The Classic 1', 'The Classic 2', 'The Classic 3' or the 'The Classic 3 variation').

The 3 midfielders rotate positions to support play on both flanks. Once the attempt on goal is completed, the players quickly move back to their starting positions and a new attack starts on the opposite side.

Once a combination is executed (e.g. 'The X' as shown in the first diagram above), the winger (7) and full back (2) on the opposite side can join in the attack in the finishing phase.

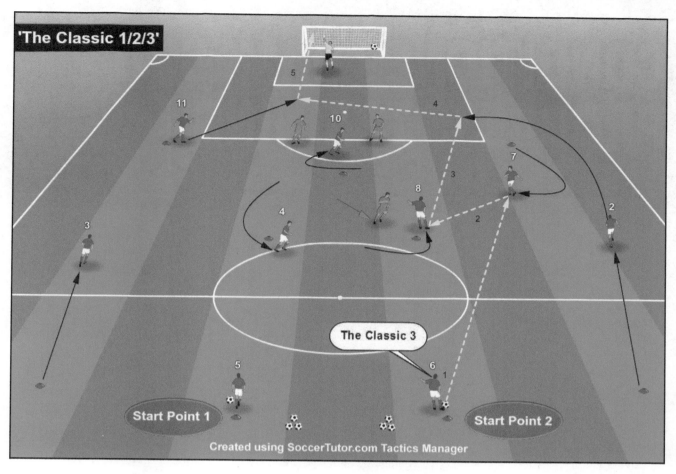

Diagram 2 (above) shows 'The Classic 3' combination.

Coaching Points

1. Can you "line up with the incoming ball", receive and pass as quickly and precisely as possible?

2. Can you make 2 movements to create space and receive? Can you time these movements well?

3. Can you show a good, "pacey" passing technique over 10/15/20 yards. "Can you ping the pass?!"

4. Can you show good communication - verbal or visual signals i.e. hand signals to show where you want the pass delivered?

CONDITIONED GAMES TO PROGRESS TRAINING

Using Conditioned Games to Progress Training of 'The Incision Phase'

Once the players have shown they understand the basic incision movements, it's time to progress their learning by increasing the competitive element. To this end, I have designed these practices and found them to be an effective way to coach the key incision patterns of play under competitive pressure.

As a rule, I like to progress learning starting from "micro sessions" where players throw/catch their way through key patterns of play. We then progress to "shadow" (or unopposed shape and movement practices) where the players explore the patterns in their favoured positions over the appropriate half pitch area.

The next stage is to use conditioned competitive practices with attackers given a "numerical advantage". This allows "overloads" in the key areas, making it easier for players to see the patterns of play in action.

The final stage is to test the players learning in a fully competitive 11 v 11 "phase of play" if you have the numbers. If not, the test of learning will come in your next competitive fixture. Adopting a structured approach like this, advancing players learning one step at a time, you greatly increase the chances of achieving success.

Key Incision Phase Combinations in an 8 v 6 Conditioned Game

No.7 Makes a well timed blind side run

No.8 is pressed so plays a 1-2 with the right back

Created using SoccerTutor.com Tactics Manager

Practice Organisation

Using half a full sized pitch, we play an 8 v 6 (+GK) conditioned game. Mark out a central grid (25 x 20 yards) with 2 grids either side for the wide players. There are 3 blue rotating midfielders vs. 2 red midfielders in the central grid. There are 3 red defenders on the edge of the penalty area. There are 2 blue wingers (7 and 11) who start in the wide grids and 2 full backs (2 and 3) who start outside the grids.

The practice begins with the blue centre back No.5 (or the coach) in the centre. He plays into a rotating midfielder as shown. After the first pass, the game goes live with free movement of players (although they follow instructions and specific patterns).

Challenge the blue attacking team to combine and use the key incision patterns of play, looking to score. If the red defending team win possession, they pass to the start position.

This first diagram (above) shows the players exploring a variation of 'The Classic 2'. When broken down, this is simply a "third-man running" scenario, leading into the 'Finishing Phase'.

The attacking midfielder (8) rotates to receive a pass from the centre back (5). As pressure arrives, he plays a one-two with the supporting right back (2). This gives the right winger (7) time to start a diagonal "blind side run" behind the opposition's left back. If this is well timed, the winger then receives a "killer pass" from No.8 through the channel (between the red left back and centre back). Can the winger then run on and score?

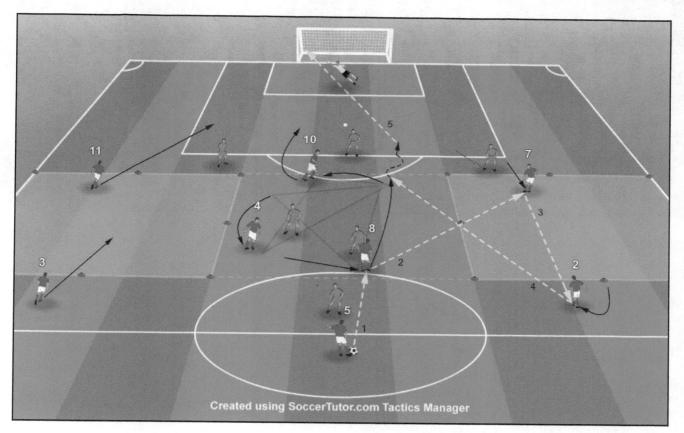

Created using SoccerTutor.com Tactics Manager

The second diagram (above) shows 'The X' combination and pattern of movement described earlier in the book.

Coaching Points

1. Can you use the key incision patterns of play e.g. 'The X', 'The Classic 1', 'The Classic 2' or 'The Classic 3', plus any variations you can come up with?

2. Can midfielders keep a disciplined shape while rotating positions to lose markers and achieve good link up play?

3. Can you use a maximum of 1/2/3 touches to mount your attacks with "pace" and "ping"?

4. Can you line up with a good side-on body position as the pass comes in? If you are under pressure, can you just set the ball back?

5. Can all advanced forwards make 2 movements to create space to receive the ball or otherwise set it back? Good timing is vital to success with this.

6. Can you make effective, well timed runs into the box to finish off scoring opportunities?
   (More on this in the 'Finishing Phase' to follow)

7. *Keep encouraging your players to explore all the key incision patterns of play. Any successful combination ending with an attempt on goal deserves applause. At such moments, I like to pause the practice and call out which incision movement they've just successfully used to break open the opponent back-line.*

8. *Once players have explored one combination, encourage them to explore another option or variation.*

'THE CUT' & 'THE OPEN GATE' COMBINATIONS

'The Cut' (Incision Phase)

No.11 cuts inside and opens up a channel for No.3 to pass to No.9

Created using SoccerTutor.com Tactics Manager

'The Cut' as used in the incision phase, gets its name from the coordinated movements of the winger (No.11 or No.7) and the striker No.9 (or No.10 if he pulls out wide). Again, this is a move you will often see at the top level in football.

For the movement to work well, there needs to be a good degree of understanding between 3 players: The full back, the winger and the striker (see diagram). It needs practice in training to ensure the coordinated movements by these players are well spaced and timed. As a coach, you can then encourage your players to explore the movement and its variations in competitive games.

In the scenario above, the striker (9) initiates the action by pulling out wide as the full back (3) receives a pass. This is the cue for the winger (11) to move inside, looking to open up the wide channel for a vertical pass into the arriving striker.

- As he moves inside, can the winger ensure to get in front and across his marker while calling for a pass from the full back?

- Can the winger signal where he wants a weighted pass into feet into the inside channel?

This forces the opposing full back to make a decision:

- Does he track the winger's inside run or does he hold his position?

If these movements are well-timed, chances are the winger's run inside will act as a decoy and drag the opponent marker inside. This, of course opens up the wide channel for the arriving striker to receive the vertical pass from the left back (3). The striker (9) can now "open up and provoke" (e.g. the covering centre back) or look to deliver a cross etc.

In training, the more the players explore such coordinated movements, the more they're likely to apply it in a competitive games. Like all skills, it takes practice to perfect. Given a little time, the players will increasingly recognise and anticipate the vital early cues. Making such movements will become part of the player's game intelligence and your team's attacking DNA.

'The Cut' (Incision Phase): 'Drive Inside & Provoke'

The diagram above shows another pass and move option when using 'The Cut'. Here the opposing full back (FB) holds his position. Rather than track our No.11's inside run, the FB opted to screen off the forward pass into the arriving striker behind. This allows our winger (11) a pocket of space to receive a pass inside from the full back (3). No.11 can now drive forward with the ball.

If the opposing full back (FB) who is marking our winger (11) holds his position and is determined to screen off the forward pass into the arriving striker (9) behind him, then Plan B runs something like the combination shown in the diagram.

The winger (11) runs inside to receive a pass from the full back (3). He can now drive forward with the ball and provoke opponents and/or pass into the arriving No.10 who has moved into position to occupy the opposition's centre backs. The No.10 can then attack and shoot or possibly play a first time killer bounce pass into the striker (9). The striker initially moved out wide and is now in position to attack the space in behind the centre back.

Movement patterns such as this offer many permutations and can therefore prove very difficult to defend against. Effectively, the marking/pressing opponent (e.g. the red

full back in the diagram) is damned if he twists (to track the run inside) and damned if he sticks (to screen off a forward pass)! Done well, such coordinated movements can prove very effective as another weapon your team can use in the attacking phases.

From here, there are many options available for the team to create a convincing finish. We will look at these in detail in the finishing phase to follow.

'The Open Gate' Using 'Set & Spin'

1. No.9 sets pass back to No.10
2. No.9 creates space for No.11
3. No.9 opens up to receive pass

No.7 pulls wide to stretch the back line

Created using SoccerTutor.com Tactics Manager

'The Open Gate' (my term for it) is another classic coordinated movement pattern you will often see top level players use. It can be a very effective means of unlocking compact opponents, especially when they are defending around their box. Where it works best is in advanced central areas around the 'D'. When done well, this coordinated movement pattern is very difficult to defend against. The diagram will give you an idea why.

In the basic form, 'The Open Gate' is a variation of what is more commonly called 'Set and Spin'. Except, there's a little more to it. The diagram shows the best known example. The striker (9) drifts away from his marker, looking to receive a diagonal forward pass from a teammate (No.2). The pass is to feet and No.9 sets the ball back with 1 touch into a supporting player (No.10 in diagram). No.9 then spins off in the opposite direction to receive the next pass.

Can the striker do this move while keeping his body side-on at all times to maintain a good view of the ball? This is perhaps what best defines 'The Open Gate' as a technical skill. The player sets the ball and makes a curved run to create space for a quick return pass to feet.

If the space opens up, can the striker use a signal to show exactly where he wants the return pass played? And if he is within shooting range, he can strike a return pass first time on goal (he only needs "half a yard").

This simple manoeuvre can be a nightmare for a defender to deal with. In this example, ***does the centre back man-mark and track the No.9's "peeling" run?***

If so, he opens the way for the No.10 to advance and potentially strike on goal. Although unlikely, if he holds his position, the No.10 can simply "bounce" the ball back to No.9 who, opening up, can shoot first time if the pass is well weighted. In other words, the movement is a great way to isolate the centre back and create a potentially lethal 2 v 1 situation within striking distance of goal.

It can get better still! Get your players to explore this coordinated movement and you are effectively coaching them what I call a ***"pass and move code"***. When all players understand how it works, they can anticipate opportunities to try it out against opponents.

In this example the left winger (11) makes a run inside to become a "second striker". As the diagonal pass reaches No.9, No.11 anticipates 'The Open Gate' movement and makes a driving run in front of the other centre back. Now the No.10 who receives the set pass has 2 "killer pass" options in what has effectively become a 3 v 1 situation! No.10 can now pass to No.9 or to No.11 with the goal gaping ahead for both. In terms of quick, incisive combination play it doesn't get much better than this!

'The Open Gate' Using an Underlap Run

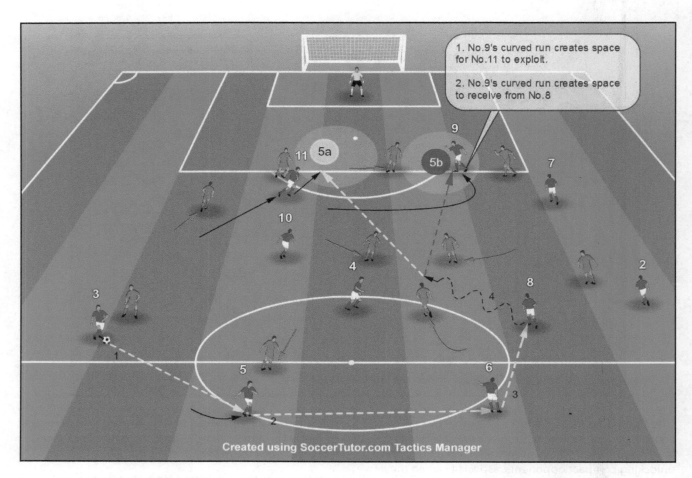

1. No.9's curved run creates space for No.11 to exploit.

2. No.9's curved run creates space to receive from No.8

Created using SoccerTutor.com Tactics Manager

The diagram shows another example of opening the gate. In this variation the striker (9) doesn't "set and spin", but instead makes a clever underlapping run in front of the advancing midfielder (8) who is running with the ball. Again, his movement is across and in the opposite direction to the travelling ball.

Now can the striker (9) quickly get "side-on" to offer himself for a pass into feet? In this way he isolates the nearest centre back who now must decide whether to hold his position or shift across and track the run.

Again, the winger on the opposite side (11) knows the movement pattern so drives forward in front of the other centre back. The goal beckons, especially when this move is pulled off in central attacking areas.

To explore 'The Open Gate' movement pattern with your players I would recommend a 7 v 6 half pitch practice with 3 attackers, 2 attacking midfielders and 2 deeper lying players (e.g. centre backs) versus 4 defenders and 2 defensive midfielders. Begin by outlining the movement pattern with a tactics board to show the players how it can work. Then get the players to explore the move

by simply throwing the ball and walking through the sequence of movements. Once understanding is established, start the practice game with a "passive" condition applied to the defending team - they can track runs but cannot tackle. This will allow the strikers the chance to see the movement pattern in practice. This will also give you the coach an opportunity to demo 'The Open Gate' technical movement (e.g. "peeling away" while keeping your body open in the opposite direction to the travelling ball). Once they show success with the basic movements and create shooting opportunities, you can progress the practice and remove the passive constraint so the game becomes fully competitive.

In order to keep the attackers focused on the learning objective, add a motivation so that any goals scored using 'The Open Gate' move are worth 5 points. Any strike on goal using a variant of the move gets 3 points. Meanwhile, if the defenders win possession, can they play a long ball to the coach who acts as an "outlet player" wide on the halfway line (1 point)?

How to Regain Dominance in Possession When a Game Gets Scrappy

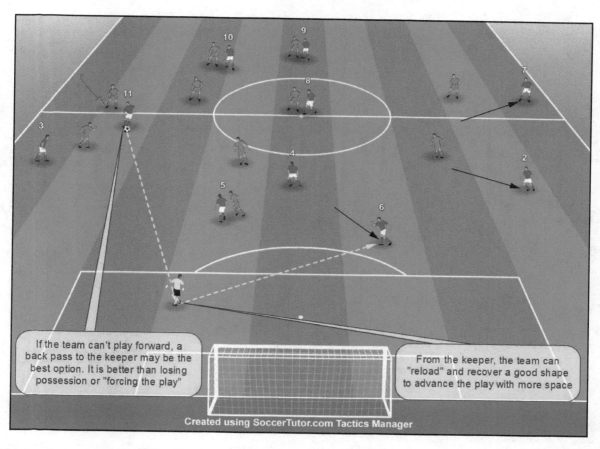

If the team can't play forward, a back pass to the keeper may be the best option. It is better than losing possession or "forcing the play"

From the keeper, the team can "reload" and recover a good shape to advance the play with more space

Created using SoccerTutor.com Tactics Manager

As a coach, what can you do when a game is getting scrappy?

When this is due to intense pressure from the opposition, making it difficult for your players to hold on to the ball or link-up, you and your team will need to work on dealing with high pressing through training and games. If the cause of the problem is fatigue, it's a fitness issue you need to address in training.

However, often games get scrappy because of loss of focus and discipline, and, if so, here's something you can try. Most, if not all teams will experience such periods in games with poor link-up play, passes getting misplaced, the team losing their shape and players ball watching etc. This can happen in any game at any time and, of course, the causes are usually all interconnected. Hence, the sooner your players come up with an answer to this problem the better. As the coach, this is where you can propose they explore a very simple solution:

"Can we play back to the keeper and start again to recover our attacking shape and coordinated movements?"

To some, this may seem a bit "negative" e.g. "we're meant to go forward, not backward!" Nothing could be further

from the truth. If you want to dominate and win games, the last thing you want is extended periods of scrappy, shapeless football. As the coach you need to let the players understand they can do better than this. Which is why, sometimes going back to the keeper is exactly what a team needs to recover their focus and organisation.

This is another reason to work with the players on playing out effectively from the keeper (as covered in Chapter 1 - 'The Build-Up and Consolidation Phase'). It gets the team used to adopting a good attacking shape and reminds players that good football is based on good positioning and good movement. From there they can look to once again play through pressure, except now the players are well spaced and the player movements regain a degree of coordination and discipline.

Again, you will see the top teams adopt this simple tactic. In my experience, it can work really well and gives the players confidence. They learn that whenever their game is losing purpose and momentum, they can "go back to basics", recycling along the back-line or via the keeper. From here they look to recover their shape, their composure and, ultimately, their ability to dominate the play, looking to create scoring opportunities.

CHAPTER 3
THE FINISHING PHASE

THE FINISHING PHASE

The Finishing Phase

Ultimately, football is about scoring goals. Goals put most of the drama into the game and help make it the most popular sport in the world. Finishing in style, indeed, any kind of finishing, is what players dream of. It's what fans want to see. Goals make the difference between winning and losing and for some people winning is all that matters. I have to admit I have a problem with this myself as I like to win games but as a coach, winning games without at the same time developing and improving your players is simply unacceptable. It isn't good for football, now or in the future.

A progressive modern coach will set themselves a higher standard, full stop. Your job is to develop your players into intelligent decision makers with strong technical ability and tactical awareness. Creating and scoring goals is a part of this, a very vital part, however there is a danger that scoring and winning becomes 'The Be All and End All'. Even at the top professional level this can lead to problems and to poor planning and preparation. Football is an organic thing and as such it is both simple and complex. To the casual observer it's a bunch of players trying to kick a ball between 2 posts. But, look again, start to study it, practice it, coach it, you quickly realise the hidden complexities. There are so many variables, so many scenarios - unsurprising when you consider there are 22 players running around on a large football pitch.

But for a youth development coach, the number one goal is to develop your players. From this point of view, winning a game is best seen as a bonus. Hence, there's something depressing about watching a match overseen by coaches whose only interest is ending up as winners. Typically the ball gets punted up field by the keeper over defenders and midfielders who just watch it fly over their heads, often straight to the opposition. One wonders who learns anything from this kind of football? No amount of craning your neck in the air is going to make you a better football player, technically or tactically. Meanwhile, defenders/midfielders don't improve their touch on the ball, they don't improve their awareness or their ability to build-up play through opponent pressure, etc. With this approach, everyone largely ball watches and you will likely get a game full of mistakes, poor movement, poor technique and poor decision making. This becomes frustrating for players, coaches and spectators. At times, it can feel like watching an orchestra full of musicians who haven't been shown how to tune their instruments. And if all the coach wants is to win, he's like the tone-deaf conductor! No one wants to be cast in that role!

You often hear the counter argument that at grass-roots level "there isn't the time", or "my players aren't good enough". I find this hard to accept. There are always aspects (technical or tactical) that you can work on with your players. Over a season, even with just one training session a week, you can expect good progress with just a bit of planning and preparation. The key is to clarify with players and parents that you see yourself as a "youth development coach", not a "win-at-all-costs coach". And, ironically, you may well find that with this approach you'll end up winning more games. There's your bonus!

The Finishing Phase as Part of the Bigger Picture

So, yes, while football is all about goals, a good coach will see scoring as part of a bigger picture. He'll want to help his players explore effective ways to build up play, looking to create scoring opportunities. And, of course, how best to "finish these off". Hence we come to the finishing phase, the last of the 4 key phases of play. To excel, a team will need to explore this phase in detail. Achieving success on a consistent basis demands it. Plus, of course, it's a lot of fun to do!

In terms of what we've covered so far, it's been all about building up play. However, dominance in possession without penetration is like sitting in a sports car but refusing to go anywhere. So the 'Finishing Phase' is where your team put the foot down on the accelerator and look to get the adrenaline going. It's where the team aim to cash in on all the hard work and creativity applied in building and consolidating the play.

The following practices aim to improve attacking performance. The focus is on how best to improve your players technical ability and tactical awareness so they score more goals. Hopefully the following pages will help you and your players answer this question in style.

Every practice set out in this section has the potential to improve your players both individually and collectively. Use the ones you like or explore the lot, it's up to you. The point is that these practices will give the players a good opportunity to acquire vital new skills and attacking know-how. This will help them create and score more goals based on good possession and build-up play as set out in this book.

KEY ATTACKING RUNS & COMBINATIONS

Moving Your Opponent to Create Space & Shoot in a 1 v 1 Duel

1 v 1

Move opponent to right or left by running with the ball and away from the area you want to attack

Once the space opens up, can the attacker accelerate into this space and create half a yard of space to shoot at goal?

Created using SoccerTutor.com Tactics Manager

Practice Organisation

In a 15 x 30 yard area, we have a 1 v 1 duel with an attacker and a defender. Split the players into grids with individual attackers taking turns to try and beat the defender and score a goal. This gives players recovery time and allows them to also observe "good practice" from their teammates. You can add goalkeepers to make finishing harder.

If a defender wins the ball or the ball goes out of play, restart the practice with the next attacker. After 5 or 10 attempts, switch the roles of the players. To add a motivational and competitive element, players can keep count of how many goals they score.

- Can the attackers dribble with the ball and draw the defender away from the area they want to attack?
- Can the attackers then accelerate into the space they have created, looking to shoot and score?

Use a tactics board to outline how the attacker can, for example, try a diagonal run with the ball to draw the defender away from the central area and then accelerate inside looking to shoot. Manage the defender to ensure he shows good defensive technique. Every 5/10 minutes call the players together and have a Q&A to review progress.

Coaching Points

1. Can you practice "running inside to cut outside" or "running outside to cut inside" with the aim of creating "half a yard" to shoot and score?

2. Can you "disguise" your intentions and draw your marker inside or outside, before dribbling in the opposite direction, looking to create a scoring opportunity?

3. Can you practice a "double-bluff" movement e.g. "go inside to go outside"? If the defender tracks these movements, can you cut inside again AND this time accelerate beyond the defender?

PROGRESSION
Exploring Blind Side, Flat & Dummy Runs (2 v 2)

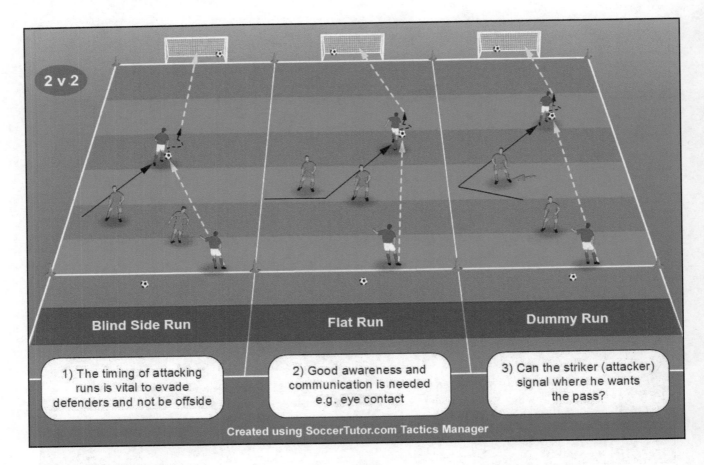

Blind Side Run

Flat Run

Dummy Run

1) The timing of attacking runs is vital to evade defenders and not be offside

2) Good awareness and communication is needed e.g. eye contact

3) Can the striker (attacker) signal where he wants the pass?

Created using SoccerTutor.com Tactics Manager

Practice Organisation

In the same 15 x 30 grids as the previous practice, we now play 2 v 2. The attackers are in pairs taking turns to attack which gives the players recovery time and allows them to observe "good practice" from their teammates. You can add goalkeepers to make finishing harder.

The attackers should use the specified attacking runs (**blind-side run**, **flat run** or **dummy run**) which are shown clearly in the diagram, to receive in behind and score. A goal scored using any of these 3 attacking runs is worth 3 points and any other goals score 1 point. Start with no offside rule applied and add the offside rule once the players are ready.

If a defender wins the ball or the ball goes out of play, restart the practice with the next pair of attackers. After 5 or 10 attempts switch the roles of the players.

Use a tactics board to show the 3 attacking runs and discuss with the players. You can start by simply playing "Throw-Catch" to explore each individual run in a simple way. Manage the defenders to ensure they work as a unit. Every 5/10 minutes call the players together and have a Q&A to review progress.

Coaching Points

1. Can you establish eye contact to help coordinate actions and help "disguise" your intentions?
2. Can the more advanced player make a well-timed run using a signal to communicate where he wants the pass?
3. Can your run be well-timed to "beat the offside trap" once the offside rule is applied?
4. Can the pass into the attackers run be "well-weighted" into space for the player to run onto?
5. Can you "place" your finish or, if appropriate, "go for power"? The coach can demo the correct shooting technique.
6. Can you always remain aware of "secondary chances", looking to finish these off?

VARIATION
Exploring "Cross-Over" & "Take-Over' Runs (2 v 2)

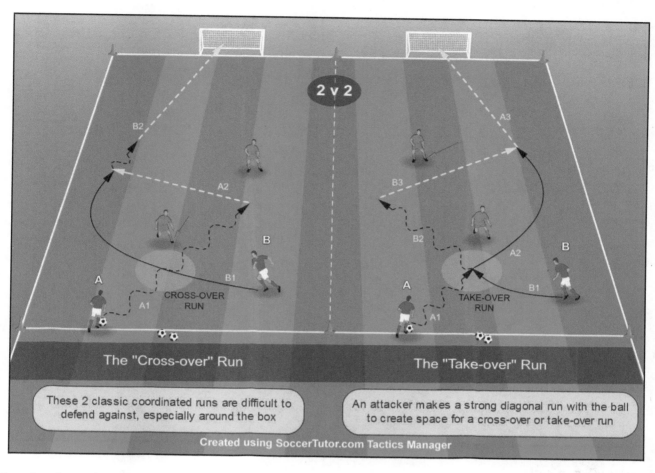

The "Cross-over" Run

These 2 classic coordinated runs are difficult to defend against, especially around the box

The "Take-over" Run

An attacker makes a strong diagonal run with the ball to create space for a cross-over or take-over run

Created using SoccerTutor.com Tactics Manager

Practice Organisation

In this variation of the previous practice, we change the attacking runs used to the 2 shown in the diagram (cross-over run and take-over run). The same aims, rules and restrictions apply. Both of these attacking moves include diagonal movement. For the *cross-over run*, one player is dribbling the ball at a diagonal angle and the defenders shift across to defend. The other player makes a run in the opposite direction to receive in the space created and score.

For the *take-over run*, one player is dribbling the ball at a diagonal angle and his teammate takes the ball off him and runs with it in the opposite direction. The 2 defenders are drawn across to the player who has taken the ball. The first player (without the ball) continues his run at the same angle and can receive in space to score. Both attacking runs are shown clearly in the diagram.

It is strongly recommend you start the practice with "passive defenders" (i.e. they are not allowed to tackle, they can only cover space). This allows the attacking players to see and explore the pattern in action. Once success has been achieved, progress to a fully competitive practice.

Coaching Points

1. Can you coordinate your runs effectively to confuse defenders?
2. Can you use clear verbal or visual communication i.e. hand signals to point where you want the pass delivered?
3. Can you beat the offside trap once the offside rule is applied?
4. Can the final pass be "well-weighted" into space for the player to run onto?
5. Can you establish eye contact and coordinate actions to help "disguise" your intentions?
6. If we progress to using goals and a keeper, can the players always remain aware of "secondary chances"?
   i.e. Run forward in case the keeper saves/spills the ball and an opportunity occurs to finish from close range.

Attacking Combinations & Finishing in Continuous 2 v 1 Duel Channels

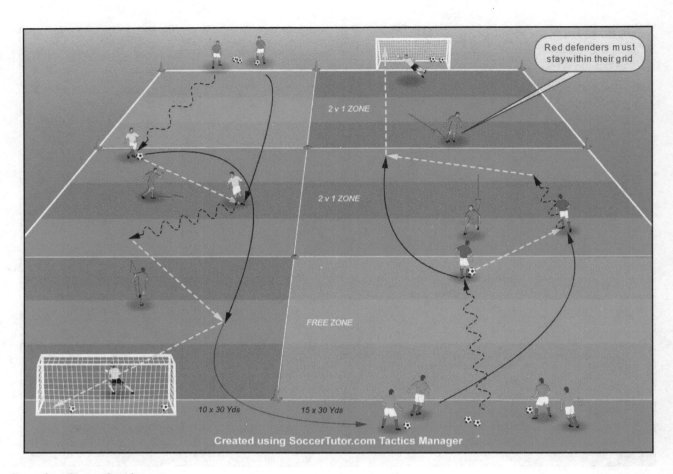

Practice Organisation

What we have learned from the previous practices can be developed in this drill. We mark out 2 grids (10 x 30 yards and 15 x 30 yards). The goals (with keepers) are in the positions shown and we have 2 attackers vs. 2 defenders in each grid.

Use cones to mark out 3 equal zones per grid (10 yards in length). This is a continuous "wave practice" where the pairs of attackers take turns to attack and try to score in a gird and then move to the next grid to attack in the opposite direction. If a defender wins the ball or the ball goes out of play, restart the practice with the next pair of attackers.

The defenders must stay within their zones. After 5 or 10 attempts, rotate the players so defenders become attackers. Challenge the attackers to play quick combinations to score. To add a motivational element, get the players to keep count to see which pair scores the most goals.

Use a tactics board to clarify the set-up and review a few attacking runs and combinations. Challenge players to use different attacking runs. Manage the defenders to ensure they work as a unit. Every 5/10 minutes call the players together around one grid. Use Q&A to review progress and discuss the coaching points below.

Coaching Points

1. Can you coordinate your runs to open up space and create shooting opportunities? Can you run diagonally with the ball to draw the marker away and create space for a teammate to exploit?
2. Can you use a clear verbal or visual signal (point with hands) to show where you want the final pass delivered?
3. Can you read the "early visual cues" and start your (wide and overlapping) runs early to "steal" into space, looking to receive a pass?
4. Can the pass into the attacker's run be "well-weighted" into space for the player to run onto and shoot first time?
5. Can you assess the keeper's position and finish effectively under pressure?
6. Can you focus on your shooting technique? When to "place" a shot and when and how to opt "for power"!
7. Can you remain alert to "secondary chances?

Exploring the Rotating "Drop" Run & Rotating "Lateral" Run (3 v 2 / 3 v 3)

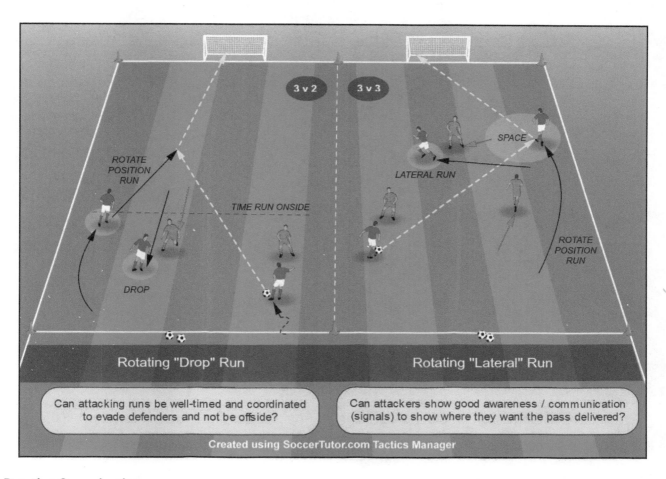

Rotating "Drop" Run

Rotating "Lateral" Run

Can attacking runs be well-timed and coordinated to evade defenders and not be offside?

Can attackers show good awareness / communication (signals) to show where they want the pass delivered?

Created using SoccerTutor.com Tactics Manager

Practice Organisation

In the same 15 x 30 grids as the previous practices, we now play 3 v 2 with the option to progress to 3 v 3. The same aims, rules and restrictions apply.

We change the attacking runs used to the 2 shown in the diagram (rotating "drop" run and rotating "lateral" run) which both require 2 coordinated movements. For the **rotating "drop" run**, one player drops back and draws a defender towards them (creating space) and another player makes a well-timed run in behind to receive.

For the **rotating "lateral" run**, one player makes a run across a defender to draw him away and create space. Another player then makes a well-timed run in behind to receive. Both attacking runs are shown clearly in the diagram.

Progression: We add keepers or position cones half a yard inside each post and challenge the attackers to score between cone and post.

Coaching Points

1. Can the advanced attacker make a convincing and selfless "decoy" run to drag away a defender?

2. Can the other attacker "read" the opportunity and start his run early to arrive into the created space to receive the "killer pass"? Can he finish?

3. Can you establish eye contact and use this to help you coordinate actions and "disguise" your intentions?

4. Can you use clear verbal or visual communication i.e. hand signals to point where you want the pass delivered?

5. Can the attacker's run beat the offside trap once the offside rule is applied?

6. Can the pass into the attacker be "well-weighted" into space for the player to run onto?

7. If you use a keeper, can the attackers always remain aware of "secondary chances"?

VARIATION
Quick Combination Play with Underlap / Overlap Run (3 v 2 / 3 v 3)

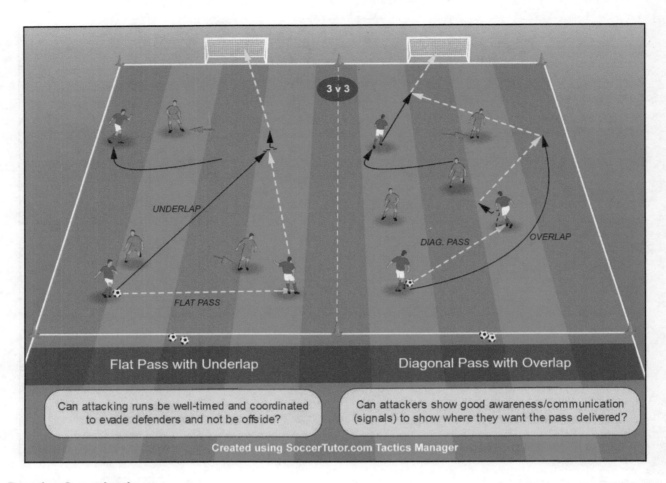

Flat Pass with Underlap | Diagonal Pass with Overlap

Can attacking runs be well-timed and coordinated to evade defenders and not be offside?

Can attackers show good awareness/communication (signals) to show where they want the pass delivered?

Created using SoccerTutor.com Tactics Manager

Practice Organisation

In this variation of the previous practices (3 v 2 / 3 v 3 duels in 15 x 30 yard grids), we simply change the attacking combinations and movements. The same aims, rules and restrictions apply.

For the **"flat" pass with under-lap**, the first player makes a sideways (flat) pass and then makes a diagonal run in between 2 opponents to receive the pass back up the line. At the same time, their teammate has moved in the opposite direction and taken his marker away with him.

For the **"diagonal" pass with overlap**, the first player makes a forward diagonal pass and then makes a curved overlapping run to receive the ball back. At the same time, their teammate has moved in the opposite direction. This either creates time and space for the first player to score or leaves this player in space available to receive and finish the attack (as shown in the diagram).

Coaching Points

1. Can the player who delivers the "flat" or "diagonal" pass accelerate quickly to arrive in an advanced position?
2. Can the player making the flat pass quickly under-lap and the player delivering the diagonal pass quickly overlap?
3. Can the more advanced attackers "read" the situation early and look to "open the gate" to drag away markers and open up space for the under-lapping or overlapping player?
4. Can you remain alert and if necessary look to combine with an advancing teammate to finish?
5. Can you establish eye contact and use this to coordinate actions and help "disguise" your intentions?
6. Can you use clear verbal or visual communication i.e. hand signals to point where you want the pass delivered?
7. Can you beat the offside trap once the offside rule is applied?
8. Can your pass into the attacker be "well-weighted" into space for your teammate to run onto?

VARIATION

Exploring the Third Man Run & the Classic One-Two Combination (3 v 2 / 3 v 3)

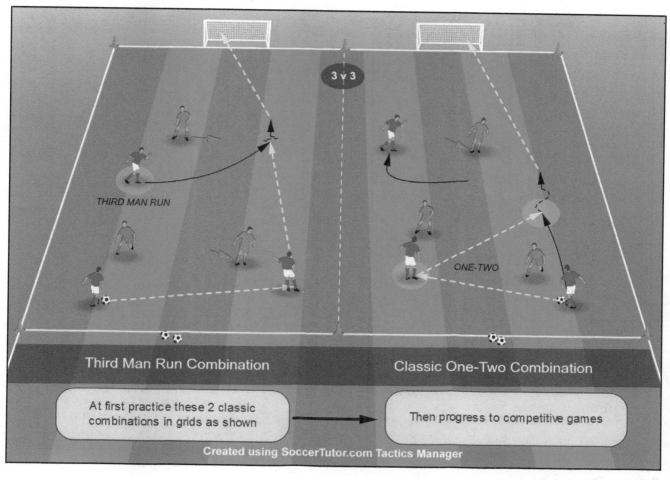

Practice Organisation

In this variation of the previous practices (3 v 2 / 3 v 3 duels in 15 x 30 yard grids), we simply change the attacking combinations and movements. The same aims, rules and restrictions apply.

For the *third man run combination*, the first player makes a sideways (flat) pass to the second player. The third player then makes a run forward to receive in space and try to score.

For the *classic one-two combination*, the first player passes to his teammate, who then passes back to him (on the run) with a first time pass. Both combinations are shown clearly in the diagram.

Progression: We add keepers or position cones half a yard inside each post and challenge the attackers to score between cone and post.

Coaching Points

1. Can you time and coordinate your runs effectively (especially the "third man run") to lose markers and create space to receive?
2. Can you use clear verbal or visual communication i.e. hand signals to point where you want the pass delivered?
3. Can you beat the offside trap once the offside rule is applied?
4. Can the pass into the attacker be "well-weighted" into space for your teammate to run onto?
5. Can you establish eye contact to coordinate actions and help "disguise" your intentions?
6. If you include a keeper in the practice, can the attackers remain aware of "secondary chances"?

...g the Back-Heel Take Over & the "Nutmeg" Dummy + Spin (3 v 2 / 3 v 3)

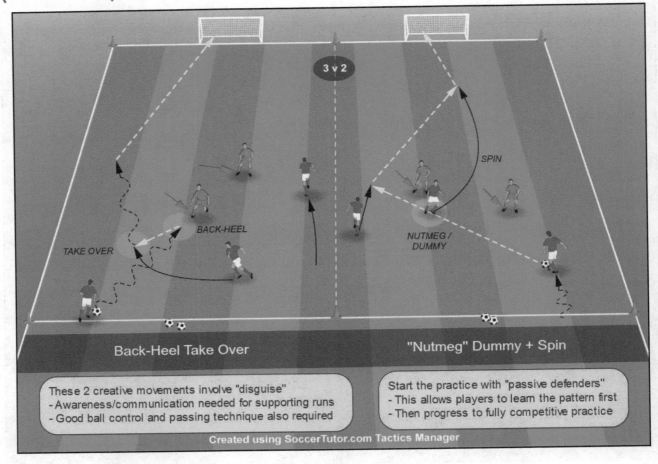

Back-Heel Take Over

"Nutmeg" Dummy + Spin

These 2 creative movements involve "disguise"
- Awareness/communication needed for supporting runs
- Good ball control and passing technique also required

Start the practice with "passive defenders"
- This allows players to learn the pattern first
- Then progress to fully competitive practice

Created using SoccerTutor.com Tactics Manager

Practice Organisation

In this variation of the previous practices (3 v 2 / 3 v 3 duels in 15 x 30 yard grids), we simply change the attacking combinations and movements. The same aims, rules and restrictions apply. The back-heel pass and the "nutmeg" dummy are more advanced skills for technically proficient players.

For the **back-heel take over**, the first player makes a forward run with the ball which draws the defenders towards him. He then makes a back heel pass in the opposite direction for a teammate who has made an overlapping run. This player can then receive in space and attack.

For the **"nutmeg" dummy and spin**, one player moves to receive a pass from a teammate which draws defenders towards him. Instead of receiving the pass, he lets the ball run through his legs and to a teammate who has made a forward run into the space created. After letting the ball run through his legs, that same player spins away to join the attack and try to score. Both combinations are shown clearly in the diagram.

Coaching Points

1. Can you coordinate your runs effectively to confuse defenders?
2. Can your back-heel pass follow a strong forward run to draw opponents and clear space?
3. Can an overlapping teammate exploit this space by running onto the drag back and drive forward as shown?
4. Can you use clear verbal communication (e.g. "Take-over!", "Megs!") or hand signals to point where you want the pass delivered?
5. Can you beat the offside trap once the offside rule is applied?
6. Can the pass into the attacker be "well-weighted" into space for your teammate to run onto?
7. Can you establish eye contact and use this to help coordinate actions and "disguise" your intentions?
8. If we include a keeper, can the attackers always remain aware of "secondary chances"?

PROGRESSION
Exploring the Drop-Set + Open Gate & the "Cut" with Third Man Run (4 v 3)

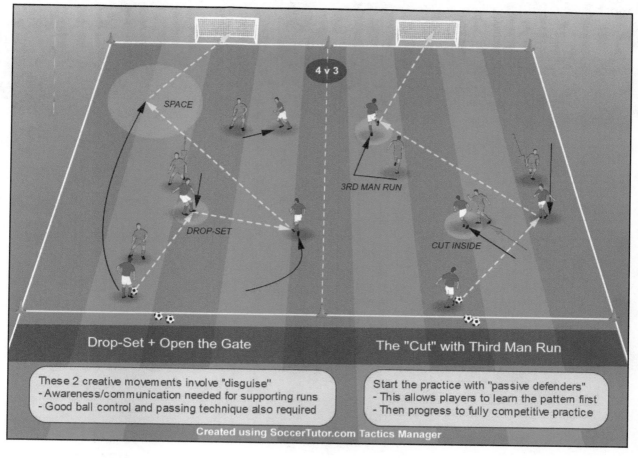

Practice Organisation

In this progression, we increase the size of the grids to 20 x 30 yards. We have 4 attackers vs. 3 defenders. The same aims, rules and restrictions apply. We again change the attacking combinations and movements, challenging the attackers to combine using these specified combinations, with the aim of scoring.

- For the *drop-set + open the gate*, the first player passes to a second player who drops back (drawing away a marker) and sets the ball back to a third player. In the meantime, the most advanced player moves out wide and the first player makes an overlapping run into the space to receive a pass from the third player.

- For the *cut with third man run*, one player makes a run across (cuts inside) to drag away a marker and create space for a teammate to receive the first pass. In the meantime, the most advanced player makes a third man run (double movement as shown in diagram) to receive the second pass in behind.

This practice is for more advanced players with good awareness and experience of more elaborate patterns of play. You can start by simply playing "Throw-Catch" to explore each individual run in a simple way, then progress using "passive defenders". You can finally progress to fully competitive defending.

Coaching Points

1. Can you coordinate your runs effectively to lose markers and open up space to create scoring opportunities? Encourage players to make decoy runs (e.g. the cut / drop-set / dummy runs) to open up space.
2. Can you establish eye contact to coordinate actions and help "disguise" your intentions?
3. Can the striker use a clear visual signal to communicate where he wants the final pass?
4. Can you read the "early visual cues" and start your runs early to "steal" into space behind your marker?
5. Can you beat the offside trap once the offside rule is applied?
6. Can your final pass be "well-weighted" into space for your teammate to run onto, looking to finish?

ATTACKING COMBINATIONS TO FINISH

Attacking Combinations to Finish: 'One-Two & Shoot"

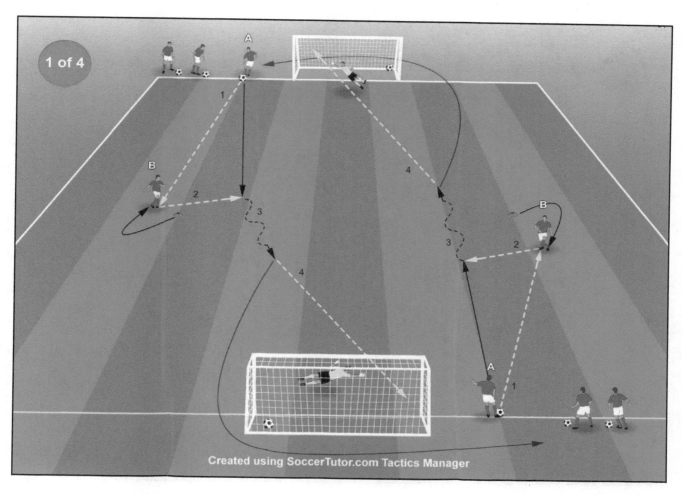

Created using SoccerTutor.com Tactics Manager

Practice Organisation

In a 40 x 50 yard area, we have 2 large goals with keepers and 2 equal groups of players at opposite ends with a ball each. We play in both directions simultaneously as shown in the diagram.

Designate 2 players as "setters" (B) who should position themselves by the cones as shown. The other players take turns to attack and try to score. Player A plays a one-two with player B, receives, shoots at goal and then runs over to join the group on the opposite side. The next player then goes. Change the "setters" after 5 or 10 attempts.

Get players to keep their own score to add a motivational element and see who scores the most. Use a tactics board to clarify the practice set-up. Call the players in every 5 minutes for a Q&A to review progress and discuss coaching points.

Coaching Points

1. Can the setter check away from the cone and then adopt a good body position to receive the ball? Can he pass first time (1 touch football) to set up shooting opportunities quickly?
2. Can the setter deliver his pass into the path of the run of the shooter?
3. Can you play precise passes ("a one-two") with good forward momentum?
4. Can you use a clear verbal or visual signal (point with hands) to show where you want the return pass delivered?
5. Can you strike first time if within range or otherwise dribble at speed and shoot using good technique?
6. Focus on shooting technique: When to "place" a shot and when and how to opt "for power"!
7. Can you follow up your shot, looking for "secondary chances" in case the keeper "spills the ball"?

VARIATION
Attacking Combinations to Finish: "Set & Spin"

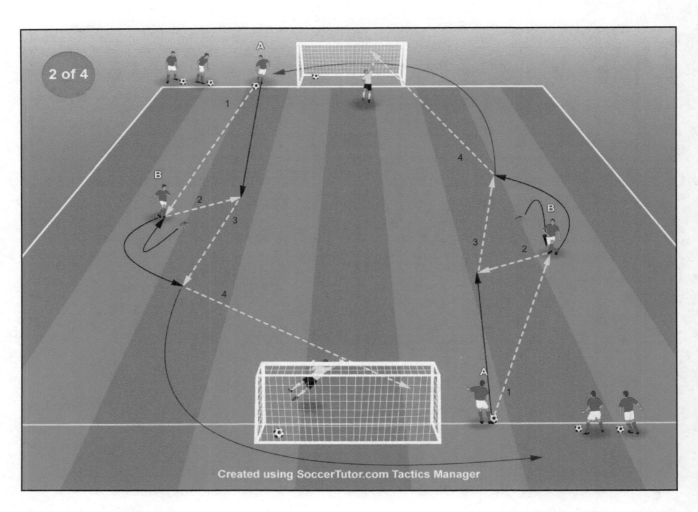

Practice Organisation

This is a variation of the previous practice.

When player A receives the ball back this time, he then plays a forward pass for player B to run onto. As soon as player B sets the ball back to player A, he makes a curved run round the cone ("Set and Spin" movement) to receive in space and shoot at goal.

Player A then moves to position B and the next player A starts a new attack. Player B recovers his ball and runs over to join the group on the opposite side.

Use a tactics board to clarify the practice set-up. Call the players in every 5 minutes for a Q&A to review progress and discuss the coaching points below.

Coaching Points

1. Can the setter check away from the cone and then adopt a good body position to receive the ball? Can he pass first time (1 touch football) to set up shooting opportunities quickly?
2. Can you play precise passes ("a one-two") with good forward momentum?
3. Can you use a clear verbal or visual signal (point with hands) to show where you want the return pass delivered?
4. Can the forward passe be played into the path of the run of the shooter after he spins?
5. Can you strike first time if within range or otherwise dribble at speed and shoot using good technique?
6. Focus on shooting technique: When to "place" a shot and when and how to opt "for power"!

VARIATION
Attacking Combinations to Finish: "Third-Man Run"

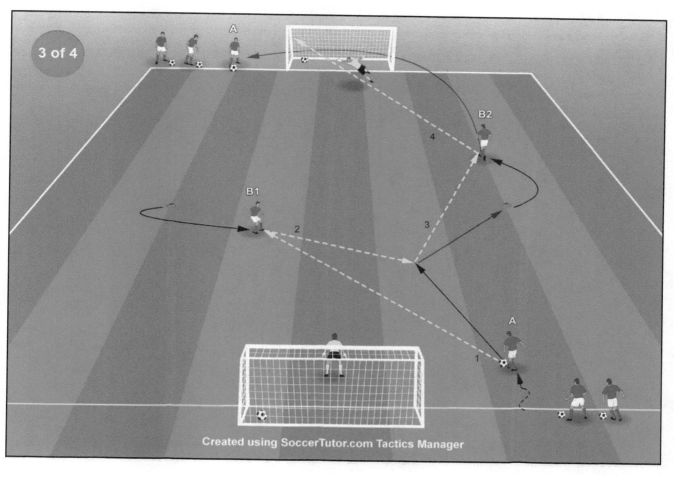

Created using SoccerTutor.com Tactics Manager

Practice Organisation

This is another variation of the previous 2 practices. This time the groups take turns and do not play simultaneously. We still have 2 "setters" (B1 & B2) but they are now involved in the same sequence.

Player A starts by playing a one-two with the setter on the opposite side (B1). As soon as player B1 sets the ball back to player A, player B2 makes a curved run (spins) to receive the next pass (pass 3) in space and shoot at goal. Player A moves to player B2's position and B2 runs over to join the group on the opposite side.

The sequence now repeats in the opposite direction (A -> B2 -> A -> B1 -> Shoot -> Collect ball and join other group).

Use a tactics board to clarify the practice set-up. Call the players in every 5 minutes for a Q&A to review progress and discuss the coaching points below.

Coaching Points

1. Can you use a clear verbal or visual signal (point with hands) to show where you want the return pass delivered?
2. Can players adopt a good body position (half turned) to receive and combine using one-touch passes?
3. Can you play precise passes ("a one-two") with good forward momentum?
4. Can forward passes be played into the path of the run of the shooter?
5. Can you strike first time if within range or otherwise dribble at speed and shoot using good technique?
6. Focus on shooting technique: When to "place" a shot and when and how to opt "for power"!
7. Can you follow up a shot, looking for "secondary chances" in case the keeper "spills the ball"?

VARIATION
Attacking Combinations to Finish: "Set & One-Two"

Created using SoccerTutor.com Tactics Manager

Practice Organisation

This is a variation of the previous practice.

Player A starts by playing a one-two with the "setter" on the opposite side (B1). Player A then "bounces" the next pass to B2 (see pass 3) who has checked away from the cone. B2 then plays a one-two with B1 (see passes 4 & 5), receiving the ball back in space and shoots at goal.

B2 then runs over to join the group on the opposite side and player A takes up the "setter position".

The sequence now repeats in the opposite direction (A -> B2 -> A -> B1 -> B2 -> B1 -> Shoot -> Collect ball and join other group).

Use a tactics board to clarify the practice set-up. Call the players in every 5 minutes for a Q&A to review progress and discuss the coaching points.

The coaching points are the same as the previous practice.

PROGRESSION
Attacking Combinations Through Central Areas in a 5 v 3 Finishing Practice

Practice Organisation

Using half a full sized pitch we mark out 7 cones in the positions shown. We have 5 attackers (2 central midfielders, 2 wingers & 1 striker) vs. 3 red defenders + 2 'Target Players' (TG). The practice starts with one of the central midfielders (yellow) as they combine and wait for the right time to play a pass in behind the defensive line.

Challenge the 3 forwards to coordinate their runs effectively to lose markers and open up space to create scoring opportunities. They get 10 attempts on goal supported by the 2 midfielders (5 v 3 attack) and keep count of how many goals they score. Then rotate the roles so you have 3 new forwards. The midfielders and the 'Target Players' rotate roles after every attempt.

The 3 red defenders try to block the passes and can track the forwards' runs into the box. Manage the defenders to ensure they work as a unit. Start the practice with "passive defenders" (i.e. they are not allowed to tackle, they can only cover space). Once success is achieved, progress to fully competitive defending. Start without the offside rule and progress to use it once the attackers start to become successful.

If a defender or keeper wins the ball, can they play quickly forward to one of the 'Target Players'? If the ball goes out of play, restart the practice with the next pair of midfielders.

Use a tactics board to show the players what attacking runs they should be making. Reinforce the understanding by initially starting the practice using throw-catch to demonstrate each individual run.

To add a motivational and competitive element, each group of 3 attackers keep score (3 points for a goal and 1 point for an attempt on goal).

Call the players after every 10 attempts for a Q&A to review progress and discuss the coaching points below.

Coaching Points

1. Can the striker "set and spin" looking to "open the gate" for a winger to make a "blind" or near-side run in front of his marker? He should aim to receive a "killer pass" and then finish with a shot on goal? (See example in diagram)

2. Can you use a clear verbal or visual signal (point with hands) to show where you want the passes delivered?

3. Can you read the "early visual cues" and start your (wide and overlapping) runs early to "steal" into space behind or in front of your marker?

4. Can you "beat the offside trap" once the offside rule is applied?

5. Can the pass into the attacker's run be "well-weighted" into space for the player to run onto?

6. Can you establish eye contact and use this to coordinate actions and help "disguise" your intentions?

7. Can you always remain aware of "secondary chances"?

PROGRESSION
"Shoot on Sight" in a 3 Team Small Sided Game

Practice Organisation

In a 30 x 30 yard area, we have 2 large goals with keepers and 3 teams of 4 players. 2 teams play a 4 v 4 game while the other team act as outside players (yellows) in the positions shown. If the numbers are uneven, you can add a neutral player to play with the team in possession. There is no offside rule, no corners kicks and we use kick-ins instead of throw-ins.

The 2 teams play a normal small sided game, but they must pass to an outside player before being allowed to shoot. Challenge the players to shoot from anywhere, near or far.

Call all the players together every 5/10 minutes. Use Q&A to help outline the coaching points below and review progress. This game is fun for the players as everyone gets a chance to explore their attacking and shooting skills.

Coaching Points

1. Can you show ambition and shoot whenever you find space and time? Half a yard is all you need to shoot!
2. Can you use clear verbal or visual signals to communicate where you want the pass and then "shoot on sight"?
3. Can you "set" a support player up for a shot if you can't shoot yourself?
4. Can you deliver a "well-weighted" pass into the path of a teammate's forward run so he can shoot first time?
5. Can you adopt a good body position to receive the ball and play one touch football to set up scoring opportunities quickly?
6. Focus on improving your shooting technique: When to "place" a shot and when and how to opt "for power"?
7. Can you follow up a shot, looking for "secondary chances" in case the keeper "spills the ball"?

PROGRESSION
"Shoot on Sight" in a 7 v 7 Small Sided Game

Practice Organisation

In this progression of the previous practice, the 4 outside players join the main game and we now play 7 v 7 (including the goalkeepers).

Challenge the players to shoot from anywhere, near or far.

There is no offside rule, no corners kicks and we use kick-ins instead of throw-ins.

The coaching points are the same as the previous practice.

CROSSING & FINISHING

Key Attacking Runs to Finish from Crosses & Cut Backs

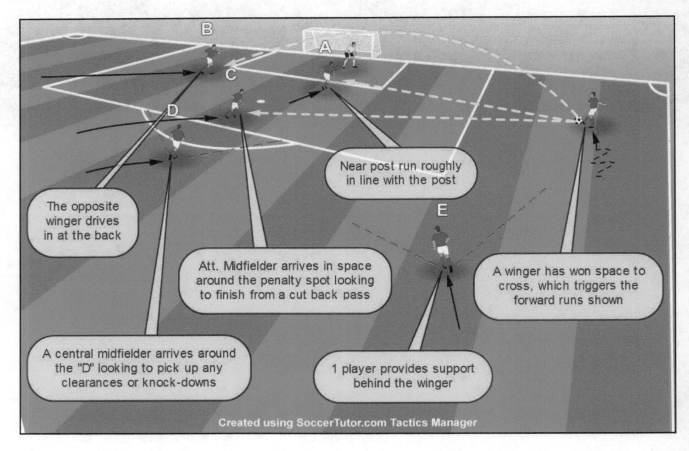

The opposite winger drives in at the back

Near post run roughly in line with the post

Att. Midfielder arrives in space around the penalty spot looking to finish from a cut back pass

A winger has won space to cross, which triggers the forward runs shown

A central midfielder arrives around the "D" looking to pick up any clearances or knock-downs

1 player provides support behind the winger

Created using SoccerTutor.com Tactics Manager

The diagram above illustrates the most commonly used finishing runs used in football. The trigger for making these key runs is when the winger has won space to advance with the ball, looking to deliver a cross or cut-back.

- Can attackers "time their runs" to arrive in space in the 4 key areas identified (A, B, C, D) with a support player (E) to provide a further passing option if the cross is not impossible?

- Can the winger anticipate these attacking runs and deliver a ball into the best option? For example, can he drive in a low ball to the near post, a lofted ball to the back post or a "cut-back" pass?

- Where possible, can all attackers use good communication to signal where they want the pass delivered?

- Can the striker (A) accelerate to lose markers and arrive at the near post to finish?

- Can this striker complete his run more or less parallel to the near post? This will make it easier for him to finish with 1 touch ("tap in").

- If he has a marker, can he make a well-timed run to get in front of his marker to score?

- Can a player e.g. attacking midfielder (C) time his run to arrive on the penalty spot, looking to finish from a "cut-back" cross?

- Can he get in front of his marker as the ball comes in? (The cut-back is typically a driven ground-ball pass)

- Can a central midfielder (D) delay his arrival, positioning himself just outside the box in front of "The D"?

- Can he finish from a cut-back pass from the winger using good communication to signal where he wants the pass delivered? Alternatively, can he be alert to any "knock-downs" or "half-clearances" and, where possible, look to finish with a first time shot?

- Can a player (E - typically the full back) take up a supporting position behind? This will provide the team with a passing outlet in case the options to cross prove impossible. It is also provides security in case the winger is dispossessed.

As the coach you need to step back and observe every time your team get in wide areas looking to deliver crosses and cut-backs. At such times, can your players pull off all of the key runs set out in the diagram (from A to E)?

If your team want to maximise their chances of scoring from these promising situations, they need to learn *TO LOCK DOWN THE BOX*. At the most basic level, this means complete as many of these key attacking runs as possible.

KEY COACHING POINT:

You may also want to introduce the concept of a *3 SECOND RULE* used by many top teams. If any attacker has arrived and remained in a key finishing position for 3 seconds without receiving a pass, he should then move or rotate with another attacker. This is so they can look again to lose markers when the cross/delivery is delayed. It is vital that mobility and space is sought after in the box at all times or openings to finish will be limited.

Practice to Explore Key Attacking Runs to Finish From Crosses

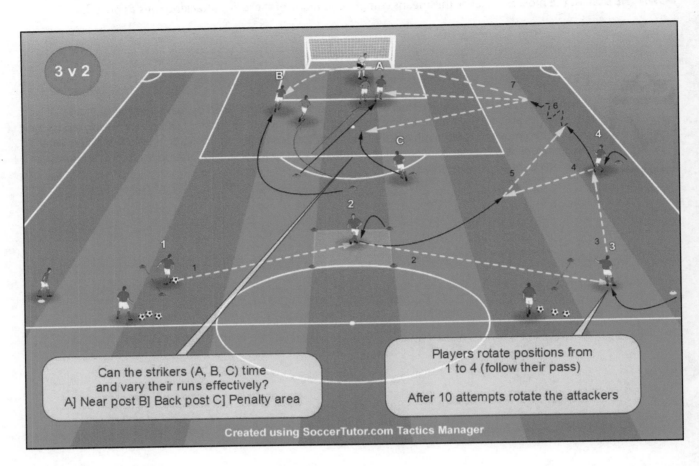

Can the strikers (A, B, C) time and vary their runs effectively?
A] Near post B] Back post C] Penalty area

Players rotate positions from 1 to 4 (follow their pass)

After 10 attempts rotate the attackers

Created using SoccerTutor.com Tactics Manager

Practice Organisation

Using half a full sized pitch, we have 3 attackers (A B & C in diagram) vs. 2 defenders who start near the edge of the penalty area. We also have 4 extra positions (1-4) where players combine to create scoring opportunities.

The practice starts with player 1 passing to player 2 in the marked out box and he passes to player 3 who checks away from the cone and passes to Player 4. In the meantime, player 2 has made a forward run. Player 4 plays a one-two with player 2 and receives the ball high up on the flank. Each player moves to the next position (1 to 2, 2 to 3, 3 to 4, 4 to start).

The winger then crosses for any of the 3 blue attackers who make varying runs into the box (near post, back post and penalty spot). Can the attackers use their timed runs to arrive at the right time and finish?

If a defender wins the ball or the ball goes out of play, restart the practice from the beginning. After 10 attempts, change the attackers to allow other players to explore these finishing runs.

I would recommend that you use a tactics board to clarify the finishing runs with the players. You can reinforce their understanding by initially playing throw-catch to learn the build-up passing sequence.

Start with no offside rule applied. As success is achieved, add the offside rule with the coach well positioned to call it. Manage the defenders to ensure they work as a unit. When you change forwards, call the players together and use Q&A to review what they've done well and what could be done better.

Progression: A goal scored using any of the 3 key attacking runs (near post, back post and penalty spot) is worth 3 points, while an attempt on goal scores 1 point. Players keep their own score.

Coaching Points

1. Can the 3 forwards (A, B & C) coordinate their runs effectively to lose markers and make the key 3 attacking runs to create a scoring opportunity? Can they explore "cross-over runs" to the near and far post etc?

2. Can the strikers vary their attacking runs and try to avoid making the same attacking run?

3. Can the attacking runs be well-timed *(NOT TOO EARLY!)* so strikers arrive in space looking to finish?

4. Can the striker accelerating toward the near post try to end his run more or less "in line" with it?

5. Can attackers use a clear verbal or visual signal (point with hands) to show where they want the cross or cut-back delivered?

6. Can the cross/cut-back into the attackers run be well-executed into space for the player to run onto?

7. Can attackers establish eye contact and use this to help them coordinate actions and help "disguise" their intentions?

8. Can attackers "beat the offside trap" once the offside rule is applied?

9. Can attackers remain aware of "secondary chances" i.e. drive forward in case the keeper "spills" (a save) and an opportunity arises to finish from close range?

COUNTER ATTACKING PRACTICES

Continuous 2 v 1 to 6 v 6 Attacking & Counter Attacking Duels

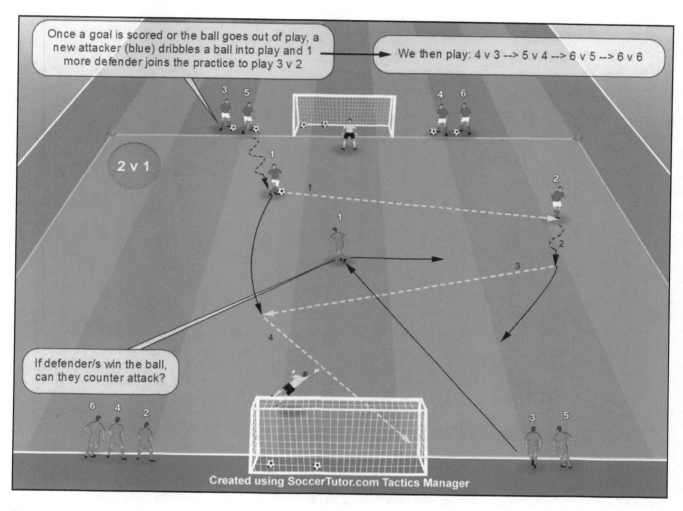

Practice Organisation

In a 40 x 40 yard area, we have 2 large goals with keepers and 2 teams of 6 numbered players. This high tempo practice starts with a 2 v 1 situation in favour of the blues. They attack and try to score.

Once a goal is scored or the ball goes out of play, a new attacker (blue) dribbles a ball into play and 1 more defender (red) joins the practice to create a 3 v 2 situation for the new attack. The practice continues in the same way so we move to 4 v 3 -> 5 v 4 -> 6 v 5 -> 6 v 6. Can attackers combine to create scoring opportunities? Can defenders stop them and look to win the ball, and then counter attack?

I would recommend that you use a tactics board to clarify possible combinations with the players. You can reinforce their understanding by initially playing throw-catch to learn the build-up passing sequence.

Start with no offside rule applied and as success is achieved, add the offside rule. Manage the defenders to ensure they work as a unit. Use Q&A to review what they've done well and what could be done better.

Coaching Points

1. Can you coordinate your runs to find space to combine and create scoring opportunities?
2. Can attacking runs be well-timed so players arrive into space looking to finish?
3. Can you show creativity to isolate defenders and beat them with the ball or body movements?
4. Can you shoot early and from distance when this is on?
5. Can you remain aware of "secondary chances"?

Attack v Defence Practice: 3 v 1 (+2 Recovering Players)

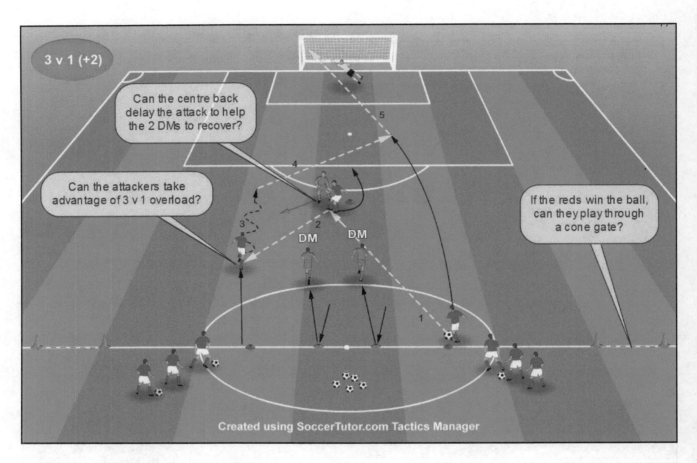

Practice Organisation

Using half a pitch, we mark out 2 red cones and 3 blue cones in the positions shown and 2 cone gates on the halfway line. We have 1 blue striker and 1 red defender near the penalty area. We also have 2 blue attacking midfielders and 2 red defensive midfielders positioned on the halfway line.

The practice starts with one of the blue midfielders playing forward to the striker. We have an initial 3 v 1 situation. The 2 red recovering defensive midfielders must run back 2 yards to the halfway line (as shown) before sprinting back to recover defensive positions and engage their opponents if possible.

Challenge the blue players to attack and combine at pace with precision and good coordinated movements, looking to score. If they can attack and finish quickly then the red defensive midfielders will not be able to recover in time. If the defenders win the ball back, they then try to play the ball through one of the cone gates (1 goal).

If the ball goes out of play, restart the practice from the beginning with the next 2 blue midfielders. Change the role of the striker often. Limit the players to 1, 2 or 3 touches depending on age/level.

Coaching Points

1. Can the striker "set" the ball back to the a supporting player and can the 3 attackers combine effectively at pace?
2. Can you explore the key attacking runs we have covered? E.g. The drop-set, third man running, cross-over runs, rotating lateral runs etc.
3. Can the striker check away from his marker to create space, receive the pass side-on and turn looking to commit the defender? If not, can he "Set and Spin" etc?
4. Can the striker look to "drift" to right or left to draw away a defender and create space for advancing teammates?
5. Observe and praise the players for successful combinations ending with a goal or attempt on goal.

PROGRESSION
Attack v Defence Practice: 6 v 2 (+3 Recovering Players)

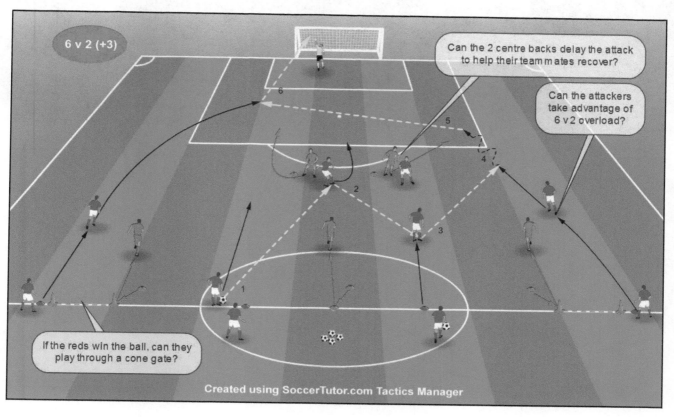

Practice Organisation

This is a progression of the previous practice. We add 2 wingers and a striker/No.10 for the blue team and we add a defender and an extra recovering midfielder for the red team. We now have a 6 v 2 (+3) practice.

All of the players starting positions are next to the cones as shown.

The practice works in the same way and starts with one of the blue midfielders passing to a forward. This time there are 6 players (including 2 wingers) who try to attack and score quickly.

We have changed the positioning of the 3 red recovering defensive midfielders but they must still run back 2 yards to the halfway line (as shown) before sprinting back to recover defensive positions and engage their opponents.

Coaching Points

1.   Can the striker "set" the ball back to the a supporting player.
2.   Can the 6 attackers combine effectively at pace and finish?
3.   Limit the players to 1, 2 or 3 touches so they mount their attacks with "pace and ping".
4.   Can you explore the key attacking runs we have covered? E.g. The drop-set, third man running, cross-over runs, rotating lateral runs etc.
5.   Can the striker check away from his marker to create space, receive the pass side-on and turn looking to commit the defender? If not, can he "Set and Spin" etc?
6.   Can the striker look to "drift" to right or left to draw away a defender and create space for advancing teammates?
7.   Observe and praise the players for successful combinations ending with a goal or attempt on goal.

SHOOTING PRACTICES

Shooting Practice: Turn & Volley in Pairs

Player A throws to B who heads the ball back over A. Can A turn and score with a volley?

Created using SoccerTutor.com Tactics Manager

Practice Organisation

We have the players in pairs outside the penalty area (as shown) in this shooting practice. The players with the ball (A) stand with their backs to goal. Player A throws the ball up to the player B who heads it back over player A's head.

- Can player A turn and allow only one bounce before volleying an attempt at goal?

The pairs take turns. Rotate the players after each round of shots to allow all players to practice their volleying technique. To add a competitive element, players can keep count of the number of goals they score out of 3 or 4 attempts. After every round of volleys, call the players together and Q&A to review what they've done well and what could be done better. Base this on clarifying the coaching points below.

Coaching Points

1. Can the pair of attackers establish eye contact and use this to coordinate actions and "disguise" their intentions?
2. Can the striker turn well to open up his body and always gauge the flight of the ball?
3. Can the striker see the position of the keeper relative to the goal to assess where best to target his shot?
4. Can the striker quickly get to the "bounce point" and line up with the ball so he can strike it cleanly with laces after one bounce?
5. Can the striker make sure not to lean back as he vollies the ball? (Otherwise he risks "skying it" over the bar)
6. Can the striker position his "standing foot" so that the tip of his toe lines up with the target area he's aiming for?
7. Can the striker relax his muscles to produce explosive force, swinging his leg with good control to volley the ball?
8. Can the striker remain aware of "secondary chances"?
   (i.e. Drive forward in case the keeper "spills" a save and an opportunity arises to finish from close range)

Combination Play to Finish with "Third Man Run"

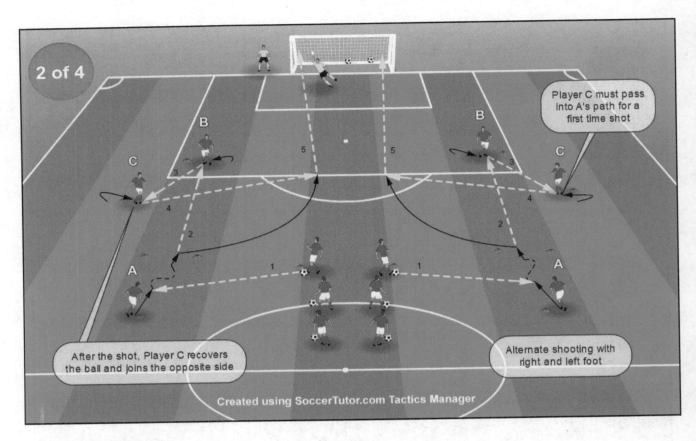

2 of 4

Player C must pass into A's path for a first time shot

After the shot, Player C recovers the ball and joins the opposite side

Alternate shooting with right and left foot

Created using SoccerTutor.com Tactics Manager

Practice Organisation

Using half a full sized pitch, we have 2 groups of attackers. Players A, B and C combine to set up shooting opportunities. The first player passes into the path of player A, who takes a touch forward, passes to player B and then makes a curved forward run towards the box. Player B sets the ball back to player C who passes into the path of player A. Player A then shoots at goal, trying to score past the goalkeeper.

The players all move to the next position. The first player moves to A, A to B and B to C. Player C recovers the ball and goes back to the start position.

Alternate from left side group to right side group. After 5/10 minutes, swap the right side group with the left side group so that the players practice shooting with both feet. Players can keep count of how many goals they score.

It is recommend that you use a tactics board to clarify the practice set up. When you swap the right and left side groups, use Q&A to review what players have done well and what could be done better.

Coaching Points

1. Can the 3 attackers (A, B & C) combine using *1 TOUCH* passes to create a clear scoring opportunity?
2. Can the striker time his run effectively, arcing it to create space to receive and shoot first time?
3. Can the striker see the position of the keeper relative to the goal to assess where best to target his shot?
4. Can the striker relax his muscles in the lead up to producing explosive force, swinging his leg with good control through the ball?
5. Can the striker also make sure not to lean backwards when shooting? (Or he risks sending his shot over the bar)
6. For extra power, can players explore driving their foot through the ball to the point where their standing foot leaves the ground?
7. Can the striker remain aware of "secondary chances"?

VARIATION
Quick Combination Play to Finish with "Overlapping Run"

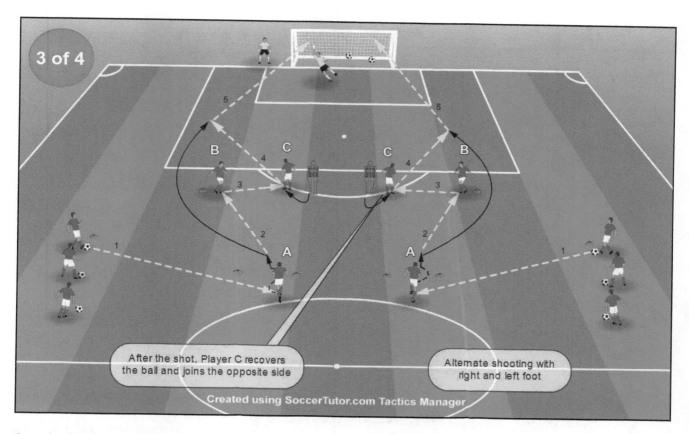

After the shot, Player C recovers the ball and joins the opposite side

Alternate shooting with right and left foot

Created using SoccerTutor.com Tactics Manager

Practice Organisation

This is a variation of the previous practice. We change the position of the first pass and the cones as shown in the diagram. Player C now starts positioned next to the mannequin. The same conditions apply.

The first player passes into the path of player A, who takes a touch forward, passes to player B and then makes an overlapping run into the box. Player B passes to player C who passes into the path of player A. Player A then shoots at goal, trying to score past the goalkeeper.

The players all move to the next position. The first player moves to A, A to B and B to C. Player C recovers the ball and goes back to the start position. After 5/10 minutes, swap the right side group with the left side group so that the players practice shooting with both feet.

Coaching Points

1. The coaching points from the previous practice are applicable again for this variation.

2. Can player A's pass be the first step of his run so he can accelerate to quickly overlap player B, receive a return pass from player C and shoot first time?

3. Can the striker make the right decision whether to "place" his shot using his side-foot or "go for power" using the "laces"?

Quick Combination Play to Finish with "Set and Spin"

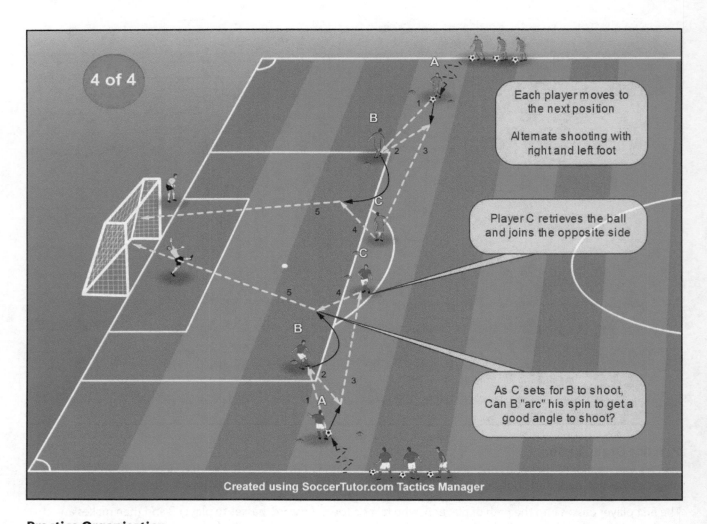

Practice Organisation

We have 2 groups of attackers on either side of the penalty area. Players A, B and C combine to set up shooting opportunities. Player A plays a one-two with player B, receives back and passes to player C. In the meantime, player B has spun round to receive the next pass from player C and shoot at goal, trying to score past the goalkeeper.

The players all move to the next position. Player A moves to B, B to C and player C recovers the ball and goes back to the start position.

Alternate from left side group to right side group. After 5/10 minutes, swap the right side group with the left side group so that the players practice shooting with both feet. Players can keep count of how many goals they score.

I would recommend that you use a tactics board to clarify the practice set up. When you swap the right and left side groups, use Q&A to review what players have done well and what could be done better.

Coaching Points

1. Can the 3 attackers (A, B & C) combine using *1 TOUCH* passes to create a clear scoring opportunity?
2. Can the shooter time his run effectively, arcing it to create space to receive and shoot first time?
3. Can the striker see the position of the keeper relative to the goal to assess where best to target his shot?
4. Can the striker also make sure not to lean backwards when shooting? (Or he risks sending his shot over the bar)
5. For extra power, can players explore driving their foot through the ball to the point where their standing foot leaves the ground?

CHAPTER 4
SUPPLEMENTARY TECHNICAL TRAINING

SUPPLEMENTARY TECHNICAL TRAINING

This section of the book sets out some very useful practices you can use regularly with your players. If, as a coach, your intention is to help create a team capable of controlling a game, then you will need to coach your players in more advanced technical mastery of the ball. It goes without saying that to dominate possession requires good technical players armed with good tactical knowledge, all working together as a team. Or, put another way, the best tactical plans will prove next to useless if your players lack the technical ability to execute those plans (especially when they are put under competitive pressure).

With this overall goal in mind, simply delivering "generic" technical practices may well be selling your players short.

There needs to be a real understanding of what the practice will achieve based on the needs of your players, individually and as a team. It also needs to make sense from a game-specific and tactical point of view. Hence, every practice that follows is designed with a specific goal to get your players more able and aware with their control of the ball, their passing of the ball and their movement on and off the ball. By exploring these technical practices (and the many others presented elsewhere in this book) and combining them with the many tactical options set out, you will provide your team with a workable platform for achieving success in competitive games.

These practices can be used for training sessions as well as warm-ups to help prepare players before competitive games. Again, I would recommend you select practices based on your players' ongoing needs. For example, if they are not switching play effectively and tending to play passes into congested areas, then you could explore practices on switching play against high-pressure opponents.

As the coach, it comes down to your powers of observation and how you diagnose what you see. In my experience a good coach can detach himself sufficiently from the emotions of the game. He does this so he can largely focus on asking himself questions with regards to technical and tactical issues. For example:

- Is my back-line pushing up with sufficient pace and shape as the team go forward?

- Are my midfielders rotating intelligently to lose markers and arrive in pockets of space to receive?

- Is their body shape right? Is my winger consistently making runs inside to become a second striker?

- Where possible, are my full backs showing ambition to make overlapping runs in advanced areas?

In my opinion these are the sorts of questions that coaches should be reflecting on during games, but can they then put these questions to the players and let them answer through discussion and through performance on the pitch? Of course, at academy level you'd expect this, however, why not also across the board at grass-roots level? And on this there's a clear consensus in the game now.

Nobody wants to see an overly emotional coach putting negative pressure on the players, never mind arguing with the referee or another manager over a decision. This will usually tell you everything about the coach - chances are they are **NOT** seeing the bigger picture and they are **NOT** focusing on the many technical and tactical aspects of the game. This is a problem because focusing on these issues is the primary role of a coach. Instead, they are likely obsessing about the result, about winning and this will compromise or certainly weaken their powers of observation. The only losers at this point become the players and, of course, the coach himself. Nobody learns anything, people get needlessly upset and the whole thing can further degenerate with parents throwing in their lot.

Apologies for this digression but it does happen and so here are a few simple words of advice: Don't go there! As a coach, in that position of responsibility, in a role where you have to set an example and be focused on assisting your players to improve... Don't go there! Stay focused on helping your players improve using your knowledge to help them channel their learning.

DRIBBLING / MOVES TO BEAT OPPONENTS, PASSING & POSSESSION TRAINING

Dribbling / Moves to Beat Opponents

Often in games the best way for a team to create space to attack is for players to run with the ball, looking to commit opponents. Typically these runs involve a good turn of pace and acceleration. Such runs are likely to draw in opponents looking to close down the run and recover the ball.

A strong forward run can "suck in" opponents in front of and behind the ball. From here, a movement to beat a player can eliminate a number of opponents and create space for a teammate to finish. We can all think of top players who do this. On many occasions, it is exactly these moments where the momentum suddenly changes and a well organised defence suddenly finds itself "carved open". Gaps open up to play through, leading to an attempt on goal.

Players with the confidence to run at opponents and beat them are essential to any quality side. It is vital to give your players plenty of opportunity and encouragement to *RUN WITH THE BALL* and, especially when in advanced areas, *SHOW DESIRE TO TAKE ON OPPONENTS*. I would recommend the practices in the ' Dribbling / Moves to Beat Opponents' section to help encourage this ability in your players.

Receiving

Good receiving skills are essential if players are to combine effectively on the ball. Players need to learn a variety of ways to bring the ball under good control. The more they practice these skills the better, especially as part of a warm-up.

To improve their receiving skills, players need to explore how to:

A) Show good "off the ball movement" to find the best space and angle to receive a pass. For example, when tightly marked by an opponent, this may involve the player checking away from the ball to draw away his marker, thereby creating space to quickly move to receive (e.g. "go-to-show" for the ball).

B) Line up with the incoming pass so the player can take a quality first touch either to bring the ball under control or to deliver an effective pass (e.g. a one-touch pass to a supporting player).

C) Adopt a good body position to receive the ball depending on the situation. For example, looking to receive the ball "side-on" when in space to achieve the best view of the field of play.

D) Explore using different parts of both feet (i.e. inside/outside/sole) to bring the ball under effective control depending on the situation.

E) Underlying all of the above skills, players will need to develop their visual awareness so they can find themselves space and anticipate the best available option as they receive the ball. Ideally, can they look to make decisions as the ball travels toward them? So, for example, if an opponent is pressing them on their right side, can their first touch take the ball away to the left?

Passing and Possession

To improve combination play, your players need to explore a wide range of passing skills over varying distances (short, medium and long). The more practice the better, preferably in a competitive game-like context e.g. working on quick, precise, short-range 'pass and move' skills. In addition, players will benefit from plenty of practice to improve their "driven" medium range passes as well as longer range lofted passes to name just a few.

With regard to individual possession play, players need lots of practice dribbling with the ball at varying speeds and distances. They need to be encouraged to take on opponents looking to beat them in effective ways. They need to explore practices with good technical guidance to help them develop quick feet and the use of disguise (e.g. body feints) to get around opponents. Your players need to do this without fear of failure and in an environment that encourages creativity and risk taking. In this way they will become more versatile and learn to be brave and show ambition to drive forward in the right areas to help create or finish off scoring opportunities.

As the coach, it's up to you to deliver a varied and challenging range of practices to help your players develop these fundamental skills. You will need to offer good quality guidance as well as give your players the freedom to discover new skills for themselves. Hopefully the following practices will help you achieve this.

Please also refer to the section on 'Visual Awareness & Game Intelligence' on page 155.

DRIBBLING / MOVES TO BEAT OPPONENTS

Technical: Close Ball Control Variations

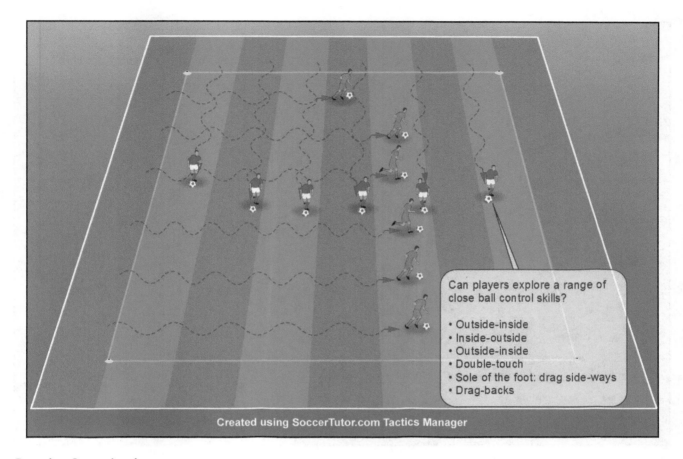

Can players explore a range of close ball control skills?

- Outside-inside
- Inside-outside
- Outside-inside
- Double-touch
- Sole of the foot: drag side-ways
- Drag-backs

Created using SoccerTutor.com Tactics Manager

Practice Organisation

In a 40 x 40 yard area we have 2 groups of 6 or 7 players. One group dribbles across at the same time the other group dribbles up or down.

Challenge the players to keep the ball under close control, while showing good awareness of their surroundings.

Practice the following different ways of running with the ball under close control:

- Outside-inside of one foot. Start with favoured foot, then use "the weaker foot".
- Inside-outside of one foot. Again, start with favoured foot, then use "the weaker foot".
- Outside-inside (right foot) to outside-inside (left foot).
- Double-touch (2 quick light touches of the ball) outside, then double-touch the ball inside using favoured foot.
- Double-touch as above using "weaker foot".
- Use the sole of the foot to drag the ball along sideways.
- Execute multiple drag-backs, alternating between right and left feet to drag the ball backwards.

Coaching Points

1. Can you show good awareness of players ahead and behind to avoid colliding or losing control of the ball?
2. Can you keep the ball under close control and take as many touches as possible as you move forward?
3. Can you keep your head up as much as possible while maintaining good close control of the ball?
4. Can you establish a good rhythm and momentum when using both feet to move forward?
5. Can you "drop your shoulder" as you change the direction of the ball? This provides a good way to practice using "body feints" as part of a movement to beat an opponent.

PROGRESSION
Moves to Beat Opponents (Left & Right) "T Practice"

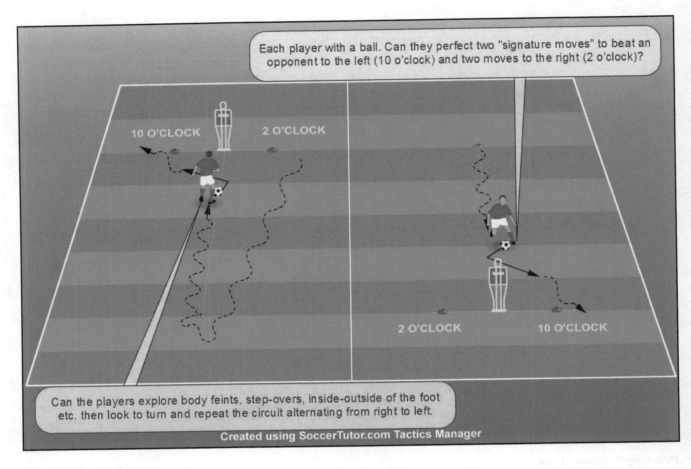

> Each player with a ball. Can they perfect two "signature moves" to beat an opponent to the left (10 o'clock) and two moves to the right (2 o'clock)?

> Can the players explore body feints, step-overs, inside-outside of the foot etc. then look to turn and repeat the circuit alternating from right to left.

Created using SoccerTutor.com Tactics Manager

Practice Organisation

In this practice each player marks out a 'T Shape' in sufficient space as shown. Explain that the 'T Shape' represents an opponent, with the blue cones representing their leg reach. Adjust the distances depending on player age/ability.

- Can the players use a "move to beat" an opponent to the left at "10 o'clock" and to the right at "two o'clock"?

- Once they have performed a "move to beat" past one mannequin, they then loop back round the opposite red cone, before performing another "move to beat" past the other mannequin.

- Can the players execute and perfect at least 2 "signature moves" to beat players at 10 o'clock and at 2 o'clock?

This is a good 10 minute practice to do regularly with your players. After 3 minutes, give them a rest and ask selected players to demo one of their "signature" moves. This way players can learn moves from each other.

Coaching Points

1. Can you keep the ball under close control while moving at a good pace?
2. Can you use body feints prior to making the movement? Can you use step-overs?
3. Can you execute movements at an effective distance? (Not too far, not too close)
4. Can you use changes of pace - slowing down then speeding up (and vice versa) prior to making the movement?
5. Can you turn quickly once you have executed a movement?
6. Can you use quick feet e.g. between 2 feet or outside-inside of 1 foot to make the movement?
7. Can you execute movements with your favoured foot and your "weaker foot"?
8. Can you use quick double-touch movements using 1 or both feet ? (2 quick light touches of the ball)
9. Can you use drag-backs (single and double)?
10. Can you explore your own creative ideas to create "signature moves"?

PROGRESSION
Moves to Beat Opponents in a Continuous Practice

Can players dribble at speed then explore a range of movements to beat players (round the two poles) while always maintaining good pace and awareness

Created using SoccerTutor.com Tactics Manager

Practice Organisation

In a 20 x 40 area the players are in groups of 3 with 1 ball per group. Mark out 2 poles or cones per group across the middle of the area, as shown in the diagram.

Two players start at one end with the third player at the other end. The first player runs forward with the ball and makes "a move to beat" to the outside of one of the poles, either to the to left or the right. He then passes to his teammate on the opposite side, before swapping positions with him. The player then repeats the same pattern in the opposite direction. This is a continuous practice.

Challenge the players to explore a range of movements while always maintaining good pace and awareness.

The coaching points are the same as the previous practice.

PROGRESSION
Continuous 1 v 1 Duels & Finishing: "Gladiator Contest"

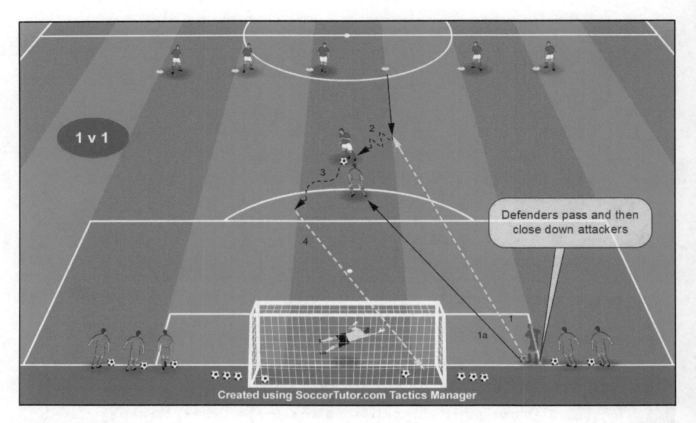

Created using SoccerTutor.com Tactics Manager

Practice Organisation

Using half a full sized pitch, we play continuous 1 v 1 duels. We split the players into equal groups of attackers and defenders (reds vs. blues).

The defenders (red) each have a ball and pass the ball to one blue player, who then dribbles forward to attack.

- Can the defender close them down and stop them shooting?
- Can the attacker beat the defender and score past the goalkeeper?

If the attacker is tackled or the ball goes out of play, start with the next defender who passes to the next attacker.

You can add a motivational element with the players taking turns to attack and keeping count of how many goals they score. After 10 minutes, swap the defenders with the attackers and call the players together - review good examples of attacking play shown by any of the players. You can also use Q&A to help make the coaching points set out below.

This practice is good fun as everyone gets a chance to explore their moves to beat opponents as well as practice shooting.

Coaching Points

1. Can you make a positive first touch to drive forward with the ball, looking to shoot early if possible?
2. Can you move your opponent from the area you want to attack?
3. Can you show ambition and good skill with a move to beat your opponent and shoot?
4. Can you shoot whenever you find space and time? Half a yard is all you need!
5. Can you assess the keeper's position and finish effectively under pressure?
6. Focus on shooting technique? When to "place" a shot and when to opt for "power"?
7. Can you follow up a shot, looking for "secondary chances"?

Moves to Beat Opponents in a 2 v 2 "Hide & Seek" Practice

Practice Organisation

In a 15 x 15 yard area we have a 2 v 2 situation.

- Can the player on the ball keep possession against opponents while his teammate works hard to make himself *UNAVAILABLE FOR A PASS* e.g. by "hiding" or "screening" himself behind opponents?

This forces the player on the ball to try and beat his opponent, and try to quickly open up a channel to expose his teammate. At this point, he can pass to his teammate and the players reverse their roles to continue.

Encourage players to take on and beat their opponents in 1 v 1 duels, looking to maintain possession. Ensure there are enough grids so that all players are fully involved in the practice.

Coaching Points

1. Can you keep the ball under close control while moving at a good pace?
2. Can you use body feints prior to making the movement? Can you use step-overs?
3. Can you execute movements at an effective distance? (Not too far, not too close)
4. Can you use changes of pace - slowing down then speeding up and vice versa prior to making the movement?
5. Can you turn quickly once you have executed a movement?
6. Can you execute movements with your favoured foot and your "weaker foot"?
7. Can you use quick double-touch movements using 1 or both feet ? (2 quick light touches of the ball)
8. Can you use drag-backs (single and double)
9. Can you explore your own creative ideas to create "signature moves"?

PROGRESSION
Close Control and Moves to Beat Opponents with a Numerical Disadvantage (2 v 3 / 2 v 4)

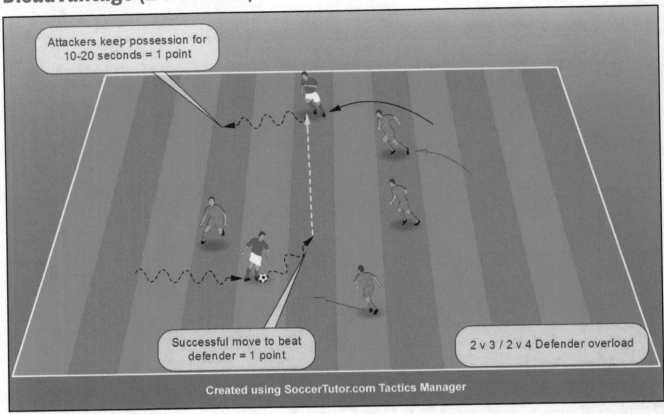

Attackers keep possession for 10-20 seconds = 1 point

Successful move to beat defender = 1 point

2 v 3 / 2 v 4 Defender overload

Created using SoccerTutor.com Tactics Manager

Practice Organisation

In a 20 x 20 yard area we play 2 v 2, 2 v 3 or 2 v 4 (with overload in favour of defenders) depending on the ability of the players. The aim for the 2 attacking players is to explore a range of movements to beat opponents where necessary in order to maintain possession.

Rotate the roles of the players every 2 or 3 minutes, allowing a short rest for players to recover. You can award points to a pair that manage to keep the ball for 10-20 seconds or for each successful move to beat an opponent etc.

Encourage the players to take on and beat their opponents in 1 v 1 situations and maintain possession. Ensure there are enough groups so that all players are fully involved in the practice.

You might consider starting the practice by covering techniques for shielding the ball:

1. Knees bent.
2. Legs apart.
3. Keep the ball on the "safe side" protected by the player's standing leg.
4. Leaning into an opponent if necessary with the elbow bent and palm against the opponent's chest to help absorb pressure as he presses etc.

You can also explore turning skills using drag-backs etc. The players will need to be proficient with these skills if they are to prosper in a tight grid when outnumbered by opponents. Once ability has been shown, progress to assist players to explore a range of the following challenges described in the coaching points.

Coaching Points

1. Can the players show good awareness of opponents, closing them down while keeping the ball under control?

2. Can the players use body feints to unbalance and confuse opponents before moving to get past them?

3. Can they try to execute their movements to beat opponents at an effective distance? Not too far, not too close.

4. Can they move their opponent outside in order to cut inside or vice versa?

5. Can they use step-overs to beat opponents?

6. Can the players use changes of pace i.e. slowing down then speeding up in order to get past an opponent?

7. Can they show good acceleration once they've executed a move to beat an opponent?

8. Can you use quick feet e.g. touches between 2 feet or outside-inside with one foot to get past the opponent? Start with the stronger foot and then practice using the "weaker foot".

9. Can they explore quick double-touch movements using one foot (2 quick light touches of the ball) outside then double-touch the ball inside using their favoured foot?

10. Can the players explore their own creative ideas to get around their opponent?

11. Can they use the sole of the foot to drag the ball along side-ways ("safe-side") and then try a turn?

12. Can they use drag-backs (single and double) to beat players? And so on...

PROGRESSION
'Running With The Ball' in a Directional 7 v 7 Game

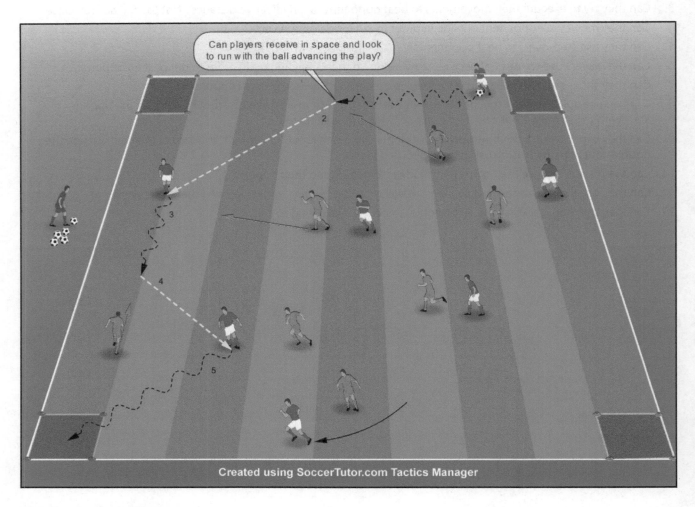

Created using SoccerTutor.com Tactics Manager

Practice Organisation

In a 50 x 50 yard area, we play a 7 v 7 (or 6 v 6) game. You can adapt the width of the area depending on player ability. If the numbers are uneven you can add a neutral player who plays with the team in possession.

Mark out 4 cone boxes in each corner as shown in the diagram. The aim is to play across from one box to the box diagonally opposite (red to red or blue to blue as shown in the diagram). If they are successful, they try to retain possession and attempt another diagonal attack across the area. Challenge the players in the following ways:

- Can you run with the ball to advance the play whenever you have the space?

- Can you run with the ball to help play from one box to the other?

- Can the players spread out to provide width and depth to find space to receive and run with the ball. Encourage a high intensity session with players running at speed with the ball, looking to take on and beat opponents.

Progressions

1. Can one player run from one box to the other? "Can you do it on your own, taking on opponents, using your skill and pace"?

2. Encourage players to "be greedy" with the ball. You can further motivate players by awarding a bronze, silver or gold for the quality of their runs.

3. There is an option to set a *NO PASSING* condition.

Coaching Points

1. Can you show good awareness, making sure to have your head up? This well help the players make the best decision of where space is available prior to receiving the ball.

2. Can you give your teammate a signal as to where you want a pass?

3. Can you make a positive first touch when receiving a pass and drive forward into available space?

4. Can you lean your body forward when receiving the pass and use a good "directional first touch" to control the ball into space and drive forward? This will help keep the ball low and under control.

5. Can your first touch also be the first stride of a forward run? This will help their speed and momentum as they run into space.

6. With good space available, can you play the ball 1 yard ahead while running at speed?

7. Head up to see options, head down when making contact with ball, then head up again to push the ball on.

8. Can you explore using your "laces" in contact with the ball to help maximise your running stride?

9. Can you maintain a steady body shape and footwork to prepare for a move to beat a player, turn, pass or shot?

10. Can you display quick feet and a range of moves to beat opponents?

PROGRESSION
'Running With The Ball' & 'Moves to Beat Opponents' in a 7 v 7 Small Sided Game

Can players run with the ball when they have space available in advanced areas?

Creates space for teammate to exploit

Space

Created using SoccerTutor.com Tactics Manager

Practice Organisation

In a 40 x 60 yard area (or half-pitch) we play a 7 v 7 game including keepers (2-2-2 formation). The coach starts the practice by playing a ball into the middle for the teams to compete for. He does the same if the ball goes out of play.

Both teams aim to score while focussing on running with the ball. If the defending team win possession, they look to explore the same conditions, aiming to score themselves.

Both teams have 2 defenders, 2 midfielders and 2 attackers. These players should be encouraged to rotate positions and try to make "compensatory movements" to cover for players making runs from deeper positions.

Coaching Points

1. Refer to the coaching points in the previous practice.
2. Can you make forward runs with the ball when you have space?
3. Can you create space for teammates to exploit? If so, can you deliver the pass?
4. Can you use a "move to beat an opponent" when in advanced areas?

PASSING & POSSESSION PRACTICES

Receiving with a Directional First Touch + Controlled Passing (Unopposed)

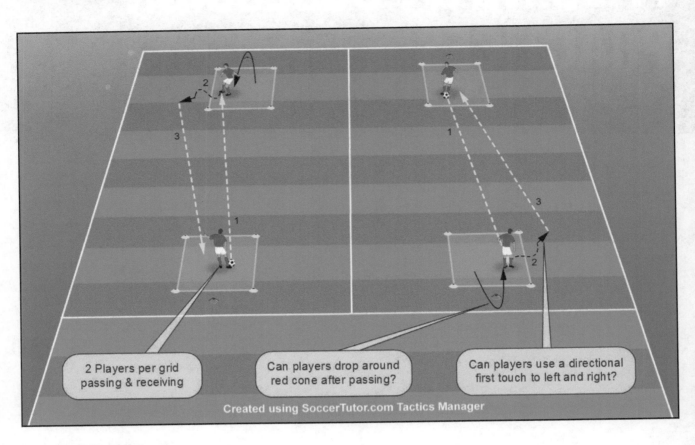

2 Players per grid passing & receiving

Can players drop around red cone after passing?

Can players use a directional first touch to left and right?

Created using SoccerTutor.com Tactics Manager

Practice Organisation

We split the players up into pairs inside 10 x 20 yard grids. Each player starts within a 2 x 2 yard box. Set up enough grids to involve all players at all times and ensure there is good spacing between the grids. There are lots of cones needed for this practice so it is best to have them all set up *BEFORE* players arrive if possible.

Players pass along the ground from box to box. After each pass, the player drops back around the red cone and returns quickly to the box ready to receive the next pass.

- Can you control the incoming pass with a good "directional first touch" out to the right/left side of the box?

- Can you then return the pass with your second touch?

- Can your return pass be delivered accurately between the 2 front cones of the opposite box?

- Can you develop a good rhythm as you exchange passes?

To add a motivational and more competitive element you can award points for each successful 2 touch execution.

After 5/10 minutes call the players together around one grid and use Q&A to review good technique and get the more able players to demo to the group. Then ask the players to go back and practice what they have learnt.

Receiving with a Directional First Touch + Controlled Passing with Pressure

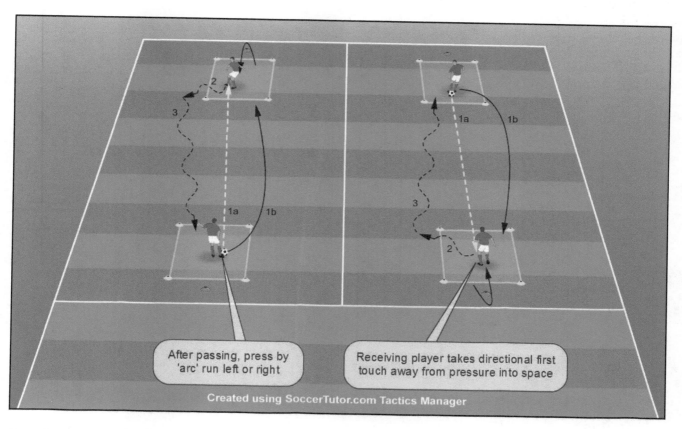

> After passing, press by 'arc' run left or right

> Receiving player takes directional first touch away from pressure into space

Created using SoccerTutor.com Tactics Manager

Practice Organisation

This is a progression of the previous practice, as we introduce pressure on the player receiving the ball.

- After a player passes the ball, he immediately makes an "arced run" to close down either the left **OR** right side of his opposite number, as shown in the diagram.

- The second player must be aware what side the pressure is on and take a directional first touch in the opposite direction. After controlling the pass with one touch out of the box and "away from pressure", can the player then run with the ball to the opposite box?

The 2 players have now swapped sides and we repeat the same pattern in the same direction but with the player roles reversed.

Coaching Points

1. Can you deliver a quality pass along the ground (i.e. "with ping")? Focus on good passing technique.
2. Can the pass be well directed and "weighted" to make it easy to control?
3. Can you "line up with the incoming pass" so you are able to take a quality first touch?
4. Can your first touch direct the ball out of the box to the left or right while keeping it under good control?
5. Can you then return an accurate pass with your second touch?

PROGRESSION
Exploring "Opening Up" to Receive & One-Touch Passing

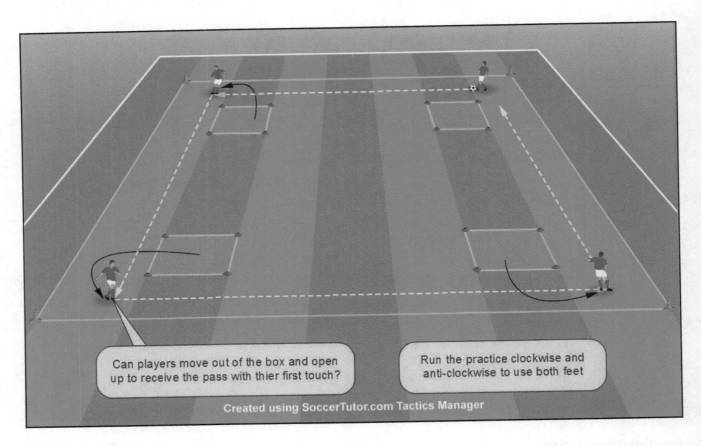

Can players move out of the box and open up to receive the pass with thier first touch?

Run the practice clockwise and anti-clockwise to use both feet

Created using SoccerTutor.com Tactics Manager

Practice Organisation

This is a progression of the previous practice. We simply combine 2 grids to create a 20 x 20 yard area with 4 coned boxes and 4 players.

3 players start inside the boxes with 1 player outside. The players pass the ball along the outside of the area and outside of the boxes, in an anti-clockwise direction as shown in the diagram.

The players must move from inside their coned box to outside the box (curved run and open body shape) to receive each new pass and then continue the sequence. This should be done with 2 touches (control and pass) and players should use their right foot at all times.

After 5/10 minutes change the pass direction from anti-clockwise to clockwise so that we test the players' ability with both feet. In a clockwise direction, the players should use their left foot at all times.

Progression: Can players move out of the box and open up to pass with their first touch? (Shown in the diagram)

Coaching Points

1. Can you make well-timed movements to get free of the box to receive the incoming pass?
2. Can you "line up with the incoming pass" (half turned/open body shape) so you can take a quality first touch or pass the ball on first time?
3. Can you establish eye-contact with the next player to indicate when and where the next pass should be played?
4. Can your pass be delivered into the space outside the next box in time for the player to arrive and receive?
5. Can you deliver a quality pass along the ground (i.e. "with ping")? Focus on good passing technique.
6. Can your pass be well directed and "weighted" to make it easy to control?
7. Can the players develop a good rhythm as they exchange passes?

5 v 5 v 5 Three Zone Possession Warm Up Game

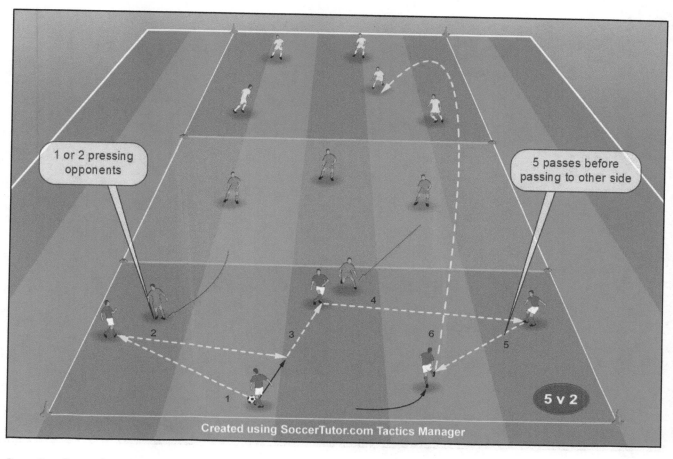

1 or 2 pressing opponents

5 passes before passing to other side

5 v 2

Created using SoccerTutor.com Tactics Manager

Practice Organisation

This is a good warm-up before competitive games as it conditions short and longer passing skills (driven and lofted).

In a 20 x 30 yard area, mark out 3 equal zones as shown in the diagram. We play with 3 teams of 4 or 5 players.

Play starts with one of the teams in an outer zone (blues in diagram). Can they play 5 passes before looking to play through or over the middle team to the opposite outer zone? The defending team (reds in diagram) can move 1 player to press and try to win the ball. Once players have achieved success with a good tempo of passing, then progress the practice and have 2 opponents press, as shown in the diagram.

If a team lose possession or the ball goes out of play, the team responsible "go in the middle". I would recommend that you set a condition of 2 or 3 touches depending on player ability.

Coaching Points

1. Can you use the full width and full depth of each zone to make the most of the available space?
2. Can you work hard to provide a good angle for a pass using good communication?
3. Can you use the correct body shape to receive the ball with a good directional first touch into space?
4. Can you pass first time and exchange quick, precise short-range passes?
5. Can you deliver longer range (ground or lofted) passes to players in the opposite zone? Can these be "well-weighted"?
6. Can the players in the opposite zone remain mobile, adjusting their positions, always looking to open up a channel between opponents to receive a pass?
7. Can you signal where you want the pass? This will improve the link up play.
8. Can you play a *FIRST TIME* pass? Otherwise, can you use *2 TOUCHES* (control and pass) with good awareness?

One / Two-Touch Technical Pass & Move Practice (I)

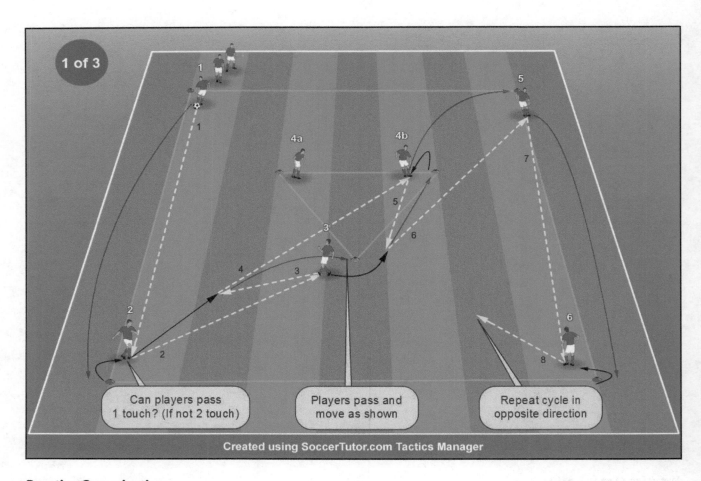

Can players pass
1 touch? (If not 2 touch)

Players pass and
move as shown

Repeat cycle in
opposite direction

Created using SoccerTutor.com Tactics Manager

Practice Organisation

This pass and move practice is for more advanced players with good 1 and 2 touch passing skills. In a 25 x 25 yard square, we have a minimum of 8 players and mark out a triangle in the centre (red cones).

From the 'Start Point', player 1 passes to player 2 and follows his pass. Player 2 passes to player 3 at the lower tip of the triangle (pass 2). Player 3 sets the ball back to player 2 (pass 3) who passes first time across to player 4b (pass 4).

Player 4b sets the ball back to player 3 (pass 5) who has spun round to receive and passes out wide to the opposite corner of the square (pass 6 to player 5). All players follow their pass to the next position (1 -> 2 / 2 -> 3 / 3 -> 4 etc).

From this point, player 5 starts the same pattern again in the opposite direction, using player 4a in the sequence this time (5 -> 6 -> 3 -> 6 -> 4a -> 3 -> 1).

Coaching Points

1. Can you deliver a quality pass along the ground (i.e. "with ping")? Focus on good passing technique.

2. Can your pass be well directed and "weighted" to make it easy for the next player to pass first time (1 touch) or at least control and pass (2 touch)?

3. Can you "line up with the incoming pass" (half turned/open body shape) so you can pass the ball on first time?

4. Can you clearly signal which foot (left or right) you want the pass delivered to?

5. Can the players in the centre triangle (who set-back passes) quickly "open up a channel" to allow a through pass to the next player?

6. Can your pass be the first step of your run as you "pass and move" in support of the ball?

7. Can all the players develop a good tempo as they exchange passes?

VARIATION
One / Two-Touch Technical Pass & Move Practice (2)

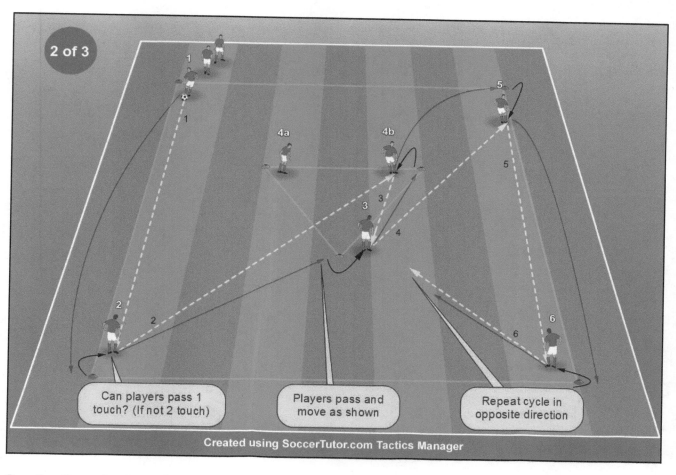

Can players pass 1 touch? (If not 2 touch)

Players pass and move as shown

Repeat cycle in opposite direction

Created using SoccerTutor.com Tactics Manager

Practice Organisation

This is a variation of the previous practice. From the 'Start Point', player 1 passes to player 2. Player 2 passes to player 4b (pass 2). Player 4b sets the ball back to player 3 (pass 3) who moves to receive and passes out wide to the opposite corner of the square (pass 4 to player 5). All players follow their pass to the next position (1 -> 2 / 2 -> 3 / 3 -> 4 etc).

From this point, player 5 starts the same pattern again in the opposite direction, using player 4a in the sequence this time (5 -> 6 -> 4a -> 3 -> 1).

These passes are over a greater distance so require good technique if they are to be delivered with pace and remain "on the ground". Observe the players who are struggling with this challenge and perhaps look to do extra one-to-one work with them to improve their ability.

Call the players in and use Q&A to discuss the coaching points set out below.

Coaching Points

1. Can you deliver a quality pass along the ground (i.e. "with ping")? Focus on good passing technique.
2. Can your pass be well directed and "weighted" to make it easier for the next player to pass on first time (1 touch) or at least control and pass (2 touch)?
3. Can you "line up with the incoming pass" (half turned/open body shape) so you can pass the ball on first time?
4. Can the players show good anticipation and look to "open up a channel" for the next through pass?
5. Can the players clearly signal which foot (left or right) they want the pass delivered to?
6. Can all the players develop a good tempo as they exchange passes?

PROGRESSION
One / Two-Touch Technical Pass & Move Practice (3)

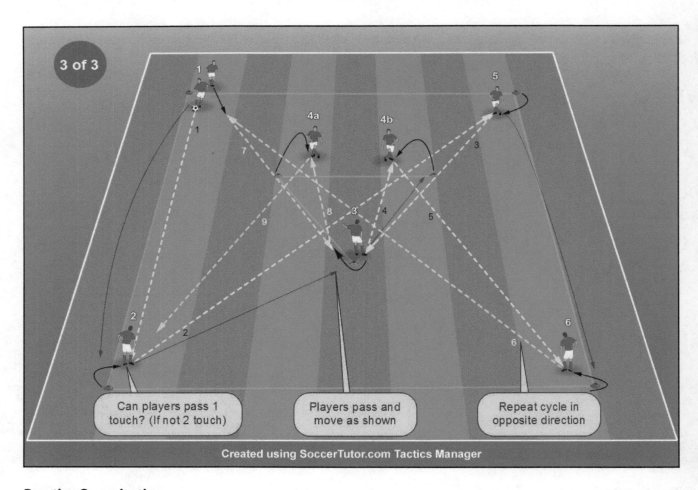

3 of 3

Can players pass 1 touch? (If not 2 touch)

Players pass and move as shown

Repeat cycle in opposite direction

Created using SoccerTutor.com Tactics Manager

Practice Organisation

This is a progression of the previous practice and we increase the difficulty level.

From the 'Start Point', player 1 passes to player 2. Player 2 then passes to player 5 in the opposite corner who sets the ball back to player 3 at the lower tip of the triangle (pass 3). Player 3 plays a short pass to 4b who passes to the bottom corner of the square (pass 5 to player 6). All players follow their pass to the next position (1 -> 2 / 2 -> 3 / 3 -> 4 etc).

From this point, player 6 passes to the next player 1 and we start a similar pattern (without the first straight pass) in the opposite direction, using player 4a this time (6 -> 1 -> 3 -> 4a -> 2).

This practice involves 25 yard diagonal passes as shown in the diagram (see pass 2 & 6). Encourage the players to try and deliver these passes on the ground. For those who are struggling, suggest they try a lofted pass across as they should find these easier to start with. Again, observe the players who are struggling with the challenges set and perhaps look to do extra one-two-one work with them to improve their ability.

Call players in and use Q&A to discuss the coaching points set out below.

Coaching Points

1. Can you deliver a quality pass along the ground (i.e. "with ping")? Focus on good passing technique.

2. Can you "line up with the incoming pass" (half turned/open body shape) so you can pass the ball on first time?

3. Can the players develop a good tempo and rhythm as they exchange passes?

One / Two-Touch Technical Pass & Move Practice (4)

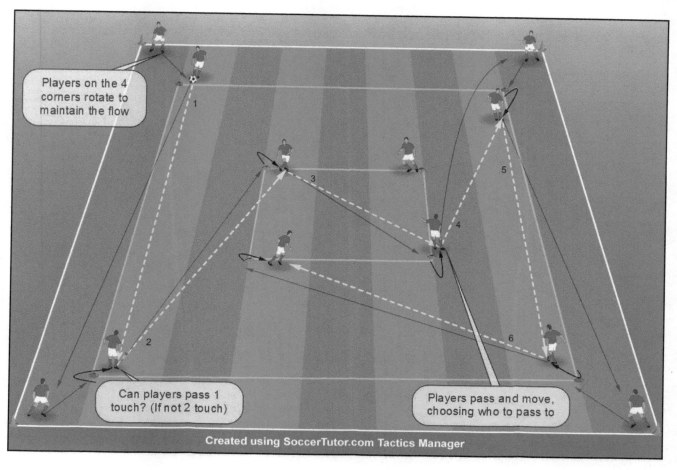

Players on the 4 corners rotate to maintain the flow

Can players pass 1 touch? (If not 2 touch)

Players pass and move, choosing who to pass to

Created using SoccerTutor.com Tactics Manager

Practice Organisation

In the same 25 x 25 square used in the previous practices, we replace the central triangle with a 15 x 15 square and play with 9-12 players.

In this practice we allow the players to choose who they pass to, which is good for testing player awareness and decision making. All players follow their pass to the next position.

Once a good tempo is established, there is an option to add a second ball.

Call the players in and use Q&A to discuss the coaching points set out below.

Coaching Points

1. Can you establish eye-contact, show good awareness and quality communication?
2. Can you deliver a quality pass along the ground (i.e. "with ping")? Focus on good passing technique.
3. Can you "line up with the incoming pass" (half turned/open body shape) so you can pass the ball on first time?
4. Can you clearly signal which foot (left or right) you want the pass delivered to?
5. Can the players in the centre square also look to "open up a channel" to allow a through pass to the next player?
6. Can your pass be the first step of your run as you "pass and move" in support of the ball?

PROGRESSION
6 (+4) v 4 Possession Practice with Rotating Corner Players

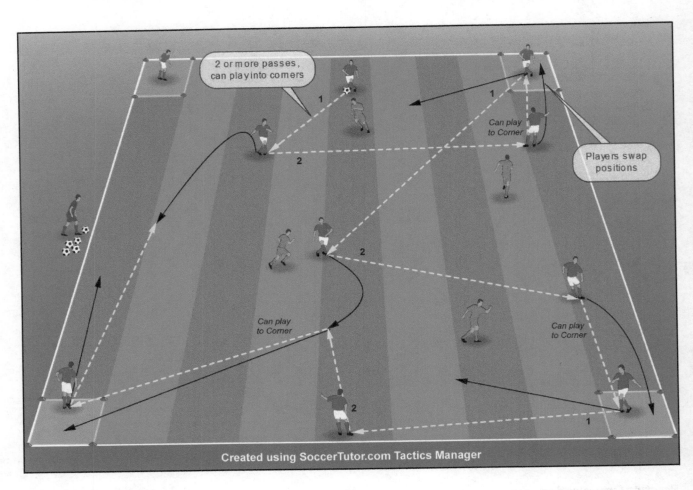

Created using SoccerTutor.com Tactics Manager

Practice Organisation

This can work as a progression to the previous practice. Simply use the same 25 x 25 area and remove the cones in the middle. We have 6 or 7 blue players (+ 4 corner players) vs. 4 red defending players.

The aim for the blue team is to play into all 4 corners without losing possession (1 point). A pass to a corner player is only allowed after 2 successful passes have been made without the opposition touching the ball. When a player passes to a corner player, they swap positions and the practice continues.

If the blue team (defenders) win the ball their aim is to complete 6 consecutive passes (1 point). The corner players are not involved in this phase.

After 5/10 minutes, call the players in and use Q&A to discuss the coaching points set out below.

Coaching Points

1. Can you establish eye-contact, show good awareness and quality communication?
2. Can you move into space after passing to find good support angles to receive a pass? The pass should be the first step of your run, as you "pass and move" in support of the ball.
3. Can you "line up with the incoming pass" (half turned/open body shape) so you can pass the ball on first time?
4. Can you clearly signal which foot (left or right) you want the pass delivered to?
5. Can you use decoy runs to "open up a channel" for a through pass to another player?

Advance the Play Through Pressure in a 2 (+8) v 4 Rondo

2 (+8) v 4 RONDO: Can the outer players "bounce" the ball
off the 2 central players to play across the grid?

Created using SoccerTutor.com Tactics Manager

Practice Organisation

In a 25 x 25 yard area we mark out a 20 x 20 yard square in the centre. You can adapt the size of the area depending on player ability. The blue team have 8 outside players and 2 players inside the central square. The red team have 4 defenders all in the central square (4 v 2 numerical advantage).

The aim for the outside players is to pass the ball from one side to the other via the 2 central players. The outside players are allowed to pass to each other, but only score a point if they move the ball from one side to the other via a central player, as shown in the diagram.

If the red team (defenders) win the ball, their aim is to complete 8 consecutive passes within the 4 v 2 central square (1 point). The outside players are not involved in this phase.

Set a condition of 1, 2 or 3 touches depending on player ability. It is very important to encourage the blue central players to use only 1 touch as they are at a 4 v 2 disadvantage in the middle. This will limit the amount of times they lose possession and keep the ball moving quickly.

Coaching Points

1. Can you play quick, precise passes along the ground to a support player? Focus on good passing technique.
2. Can the central players make 2 movements (check away before moving to receive) to create space to receive a pass? Can they also signal where they want the pass delivered?
3. Can all players (including outer players) pass and move to find a good support angle to receive a pass?
4. Can you establish eye-contact, show good awareness and quality communication?
5. Can the central players "bounce" the pass first time to a support player?

PROGRESSION
Switching Play Against High Intensity Pressure in a Possession Game with Target Players

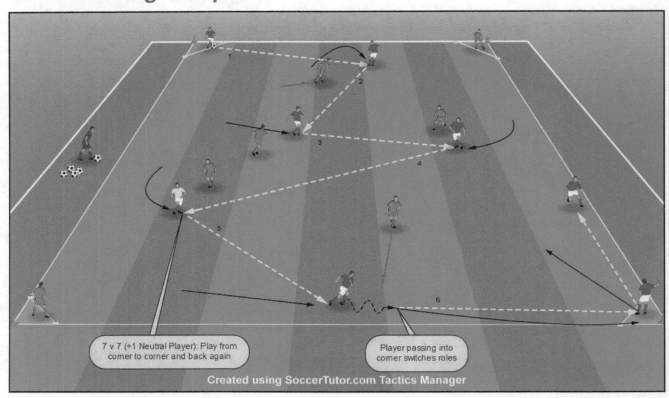

7 v 7 (+1 Neutral Player): Play from corner to corner and back again

Player passing into corner switches roles

Created using SoccerTutor.com Tactics Manager

Practice Organisation

In a 40 x 50 yard area we play 7 v 7 (or 6 v 6) + 1 neutral player (yellow) who plays with the team in possession. You can adapt the width of the area depending on player ability. Mark out 4 cone gates (target goals) in each corner with 2 target players on each team positioned in opposite diagonal goals.

Challenge the teams to switch play from one of their target players to the other. The player who passes to the target player swaps position with him.

Start by challenging players to switch play while keeping the ball on the ground. You can then progress the practice by challenging the players to use longer lofted passes.

I would recommend that you set a condition of 2 or 3 touches depending on player ability.

Coaching Points

1. Can you spread out as a team and provide good width/depth to attack and switch play?
2. Can you quickly form effective triangles to offer support angles to receive and progress the play?
3. Can you show good awareness and play positive penetrating passes to quickly switch play?
4. Can you use quick, precise, driven passes along the ground?
5. Can you use quick, precise, driven lofted passes?
6. Can you signal where you want the pass delivered?
7. Can you play a *FIRST TIME* pass? Otherwise, can you use *2 TOUCHES* with good technique, "opening up" to receive and then pass with good awareness of supporting teammates near and far?

Creating Space to Finish in a 4 v 4 (+5) Possession Practice

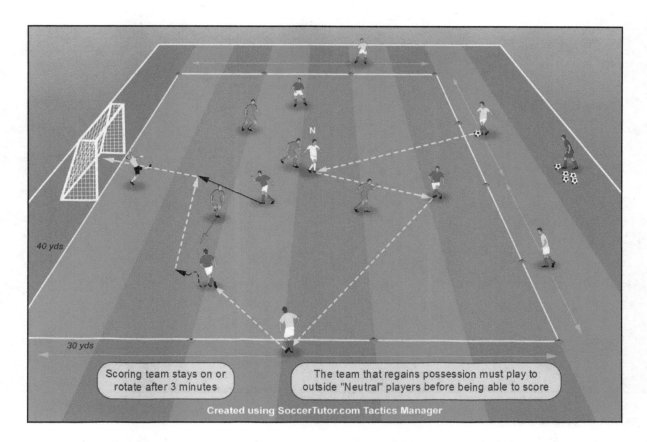

40 yds

30 yds

| Scoring team stays on or rotate after 3 minutes | The team that regains possession must play to outside "Neutral" players before being able to score |

Created using SoccerTutor.com Tactics Manager

Practice Organisation

In a 30 x 40 yard area we have 3 teams of 4 players, a keeper and 1 neutral player (white). 2 of the teams compete inside the area. The team in possession are supported by 4 players outside the area (yellow team in diagram) and 1 neutral player (inside) as they try to create space to shoot. The neutral player and the outside yellow players are not allowed to score.

The practice starts when an outside player passes into the area. The team in possession (blues) aim to exploit their support and try to score in the goal. If the defending team win the ball, they become the attacking team and the attacking team become the defending team.

We play 3 minute games. Rotate the teams so each team competes inside for 2 games. I would recommend that you set a condition of 2 or 3 touches depending on player ability.

- Can the players find small spaces and angles to "get shots off"? If they have space/time to shoot, then they can shoot from anywhere in the area.

- If the shot is not on, can the players combine with supporting players to create an opportunity for a teammate?

Coaching Points

1. Challenge the players to use the full width (e.g. outside players), depth and mobility to drag away markers and create shooting opportunities.

2. When shots are "NOT ON", can you execute quick/precise passes along the ground to combine with teammates?

3. Can you make 2 movements (check away before moving to receive) and signal where you want the pass delivered?

4. Can you pass into a striker and follow the pass? Call out "set me" and then shoot on sight if the pass back is weighted well.

5. Call the players together and use Q&A to discuss the finer detail on good power-shooting technique.

Playing Through the Thirds with Two-Way Pressure in a Zonal Possession Game

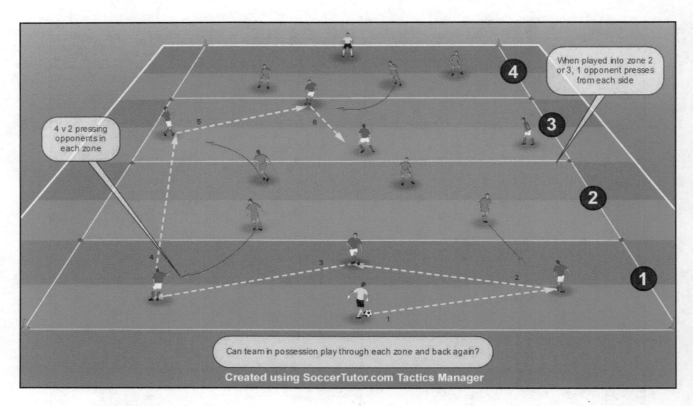

Practice Organisation

In a 25 x 30 yard area, mark out 4 equal zones as shown in the diagram. We play 8 v 8 (or 6 v 6) including keepers. Each team is split into groups of 3 or 4 and occupy different zones.

Play starts with one team. Can they play 2 or 3 passes before looking to play to their teammates in another zone? The defending team (reds in diagram) move 2 players from the adjoining zone/s to press and try to win the ball (this can be 1 from each zone if the ball is in grid 2 or 3). The diagram shows the blue team passing from zone 1 to 3.

Challenge the players to "play from zone to zone" as many times as possible using ground passes.

If the defending team win the ball, they then look to play from zone to zone and the team that lost the ball look to press and win the ball back. If the ball goes out of play, the team which lost possession forfeit the ball to their opponents. I would recommend that you set a condition of 2 or 3 touches depending on player ability.

Coaching Points

1. Can you use the full width and full depth of each zone to make the most of the available space?
2. Can you work hard to provide a good angle for a pass? Can you communicate well?
3. Can you adopt a good body position to receive the ball and use a good directional first touch into space?
4. Can you pass first time and exchange quick, precise short-range passes?
5. Can you deliver "well-weighted" precise driven passes along the ground to teammates in the other zone?
6. Can you play a *FIRST TIME* pass? Otherwise, can you use *2 TOUCHES* with good awareness to control & pass?
7. Can the players in other zones remain mobile, adjusting positions to open up channels and receive?

Playing Through the Thirds in a 6 v 3 / 8 v 4 Zonal Game

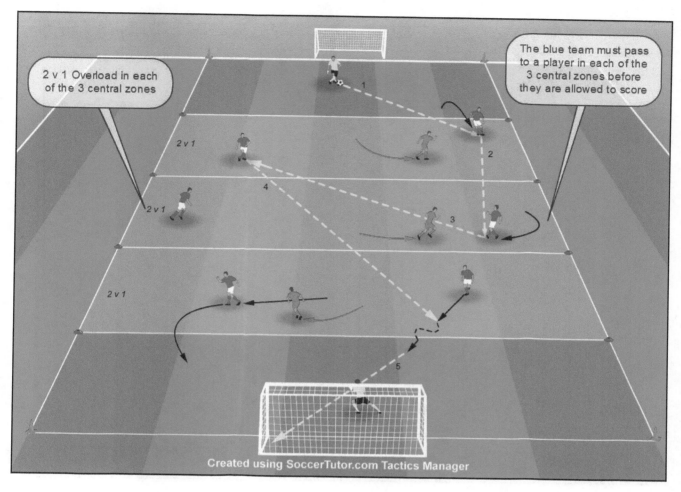

> 2 v 1 Overload in each of the 3 central zones

> The blue team must pass to a player in each of the 3 central zones before they are allowed to score

Created using SoccerTutor.com Tactics Manager

Practice Organisation

In a 30 x 50 yard area, we play a 6 v 3 (or 8 v 4) game + 2 goalkeepers. You can adjust the width of the area depending on player ability. The area is marked out into 5 equal zones (10 yards) as shown in the diagram. There is a 2 v 1 numerical advantage (overload) for the blue attacking team in each of the 3 central zones.

The practice starts with the keeper who passes to a blue player in the nearest zone. The aim for the blue team is to "play through the thirds" using ground passes, before trying to shoot and score once in the final zone.

The blue team must pass to a player in each of the 3 central zones before they are allowed to enter the final zone and try to score. However, the players are allowed to pass backwards as they aim to "play through the thirds". Rotate the players' positions/roles often. You can set a condition of 2 or 3 touches depending on player ability.

Progression: Try 2 v 2 in each zone or widen the area and play 3 v 2 in favour of the attackers.

Coaching Points

1. Can you exploit the width of the zones to make the most of the 2 v 1 advantage?
2. Try to play quick, precise, driven passes along the ground to your teammates.
3. Challenge players to make 2 movements (check away before moving to receive) and also signal where they want the pass delivered.
4. Can you play a *FIRST TIME* pass? Otherwise, can you use *2 TOUCHES* with good technique?
5. Can you "open up" to receive and then pass with good awareness of supporting teammates?

Possession, Crossing & Finishing in a Small Sided Game with Side Zones

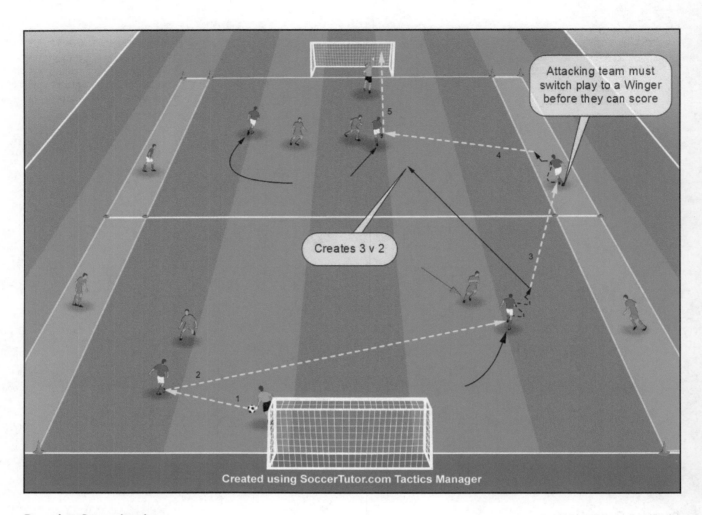

Practice Organisation

In a 50 x 60 yard area, we play a 7 v 7 small sided game. You can adapt the width of the area depending on player ability. Mark out the halfway line and 2 wide channels as shown in the diagram. There is a 2 v 2 situation in each half as shown. Each team also have 2 unopposed wingers in the wide channels. The practice starts with the keeper.

The aim is to score but the teams must play through a winger (limited to 2 touches) who should look to cross or provide cut backs for teammates to finish. Once the ball is played into the winger, 1 player from the defensive half can move into the attacking half to join the 2 attackers, creating a 3 v 2 attacking overload.

Once progress is shown, you can rotate the wide players. I would recommend that you set a condition of 2 or 3 touches for the central players, depending on player ability.

Progression: The winger on the opposite side can join the attack looking to finish at the far post (4 v 2 attack).

Coaching Points

1. Can you make movements to drag away markers and open up space for teammates?
2. Can you release the wide players quickly with driven or lofted passes and then provide quick support?
3. Can you make the key attacking runs looking to finish at 1) the near post 2) the far post 3) around the penalty spot 4) or arriving from deep from a cut-back?
4. Can the winger anticipate these runs and play the right pass e.g. driven in, lofted or cut-back with precision?
5. When there is a delay in delivering the cross, can the attackers apply the "3 second rule" and adjust their positions to lose markers? *(See page 103 'KEY COACHING POINT' for full explanation).*

CHAPTER 5
SET PIECES

WHY USE SHORT CORNERS / FREE KICKS?

This section just gives a flavour of the ideas you can explore around taking short corners and free kicks. There are of course so many variations it is impossible to include all of them in this chapter. What follows are simply a few scenarios that may help to provoke the imagination. If these encourage you as a coach to work with your players on your own ideas with the aim of exploring these in practice and competitive games, then what follows will have served its purpose!

One thing I would emphasise is that *if you favour possession football then you will need to take this aspect of the game seriously.* For example, when taking corners, there is a lot of potential to create scoring opportunities, so it deserves your attention. Simply "lumping it in" hoping players will finish off any chances with their head or feet arguably belongs to another philosophical view of the game. If maintaining possession is your mantra of choice, then you will want to get more from such promising situations. Simply "drilling it in" also presents your team with dangers, namely, a quick counter attack from the opposition. All it takes is a strong headed clearance and your team not only forfeit possession but also, in transition to defence, you are potentially "very disorganised as the opposition look to counter attack from deep. In other words, a corner can be as dangerous as it can be promising!

In a recent academy game the opposition team responded to us being awarded a corner by pushing 4 of their attackers up to the halfway line. I left my players to deal with this problem for themselves. As a consequence, the entire back 4 elected to stay back in order to man-mark the 4 attackers. This meant a potential 4 v 4 scenario - clearly an advantage for the attacking team if the ball could be delivered in to them. Meanwhile, in and around their area, as we prepared to take our corner this created a 6 v 6 scenario (not including their keeper). Here surely was a perfect opportunity for us to explore a short corner option, keeping possession to improve our chances of creating a gilt-edged scoring opportunity. By contrast, "lumping it in" would represent a 50-50 scenario or worse if you include their keeper.

In this situation, our players made the wrong decision. No one offered themselves to "go short" and so the corner taker "went long". The opposition cleared the cross easily and one of their midfielders was soon charging forward into space and played a lofted pass to turn our back 4 and release their 4 attackers. From here one of these strikers ran through for a 1 v 1 with our keeper. What had begun as a promising chance for us to score from a corner had become a great scoring opportunity for the opposition!

On the day we were fortunate to have a keeper quick on his feet who narrowed the angle and pulled off a great block. When I got the players in and we discussed this moment in the game, they all knew they had perhaps made the wrong decision. Going long from the corner when faced with 4 opposing attackers pushed up was an unnecessary gamble. Had the team gone short and explored one of our "corner patterns", chances are we would have maintained more control of the situation (especially as they had a tall back 4!). This would have allowed us a greater chance to craft a scoring opportunity and arguably the potential for a more balanced defensive recovery if the ball was lost.

So the choice is yours, but given the time, I would always recommend you explore a few "short corner options" with your team. What follows are just a few basic ideas you might like to try. There are, no doubt, many more out there if you care to look.

Short Corner Routine: "Sole Roll & Scoop"

No.8 has two good options:
1) Cut back to the No. 4
2) Drive a pass into No.10
3) Lofted pass to the back post

No.7 scoops the ball over pressing defenders into the run of No.8

Created using SoccerTutor.com Tactics Manager

Here is an example of a creative short corner. It is one of many you can look to explore with your team. This example requires a good use of "disguise" with a degree of technical ability, followed by good coordinated movements to finish.

2 attackers stand next to the ball as if they are deciding who will take the corner kick. Chances are this will attract 2 opponents (see diagram) to cover space and deter a short corner. Meanwhile, the team prepare for a pass/cross into the penalty area. There is also a player (No.3 in diagram) who runs to cover the 'D' looking to intercept any clearances and shoot at goal.

For security the attacking team (blue) keep a full back (No.2 in diagram) in a supporting position on the same side as the corner. This will likely draw away an additional defender, leaving more space to attack inside the box. In addition, 2 defenders (5 & 6) stay back to cover the attacker who has remained up.

HOW IT WORKS: One of the 2 corner takers rolls the ball forward with the sole of his foot and then runs around or between the 2 pressing opponents. His teammate *SCOOPS* the ball over the 2 opponents into his path.

From here, can this player control the ball and pick his pass looking for the following?

1. Cut-back pass to any of the players arriving in space inside the box. This is often around the penalty spot or the 'D'.

2. Play into the near post (No.10's run in diagram).

3. Chip the ball to the back post where 1 or 2 attackers should look to try and finish with a header. No.9 makes this run in the diagram.

This short corner benefits from the element of surprise. It also draws a number of defenders away from the box. This leaves a lot more space for attackers to make runs. It challenges the players to use "disguise" to conceal their intentions. It requires a number of coordinated movements, allowing players to explore all the key finishing runs. And last but not least, the team retain a reasonable degree of security if the opposition clear the ball. From this point of view, you begin to appreciate the benefits of short corners. If the key for you and your players is development and learning, then there's much to be gained from exploring short corners such as this one.

Short Corner Routine: "Set & Spin"

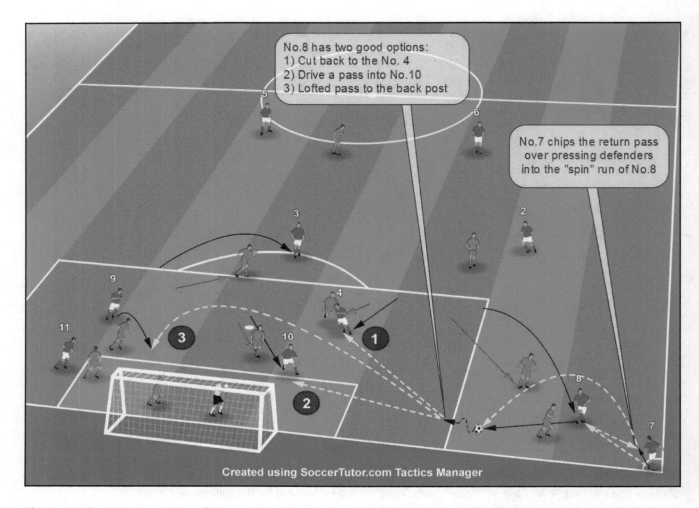

No.8 has two good options:
1) Cut back to the No. 4
2) Drive a pass into No.10
3) Lofted pass to the back post

No.7 chips the return pass over pressing defenders into the "spin" run of No.8

Created using SoccerTutor.com Tactics Manager

The "set and spin" is a variation of the previous short corner. It is also very creative in its use of disguise and skillful link-up play.

No.8 makes a late run towards the corner flag. The chances are his run will be tracked by an opponent and there may also be a second opponent who will quickly close him down to avoid a 2 v 1 situation occurring from the corner.

Using eye-contact and good "disguise", the corner taker (No.7) plays a short pass into No.8's path. With pressure behind him, No.8 "sets" the ball back to the corner taker and immediately "spins" around or between the 2 opposition players. The corner taker then chips the return pass into No.8's run.

From here, can this player control the ball and pick his pass looking for the following?

1. Cut-back pass to any of the players arriving in space inside the box. This is often around the penalty spot or the 'D'.

2. Play into the near post (No.10's run in diagram).

3. Chip the ball to the back post where 1 or 2 attackers should look to try and finish with a header. No.9 makes this run in the diagram.

Short Corner Routine: "One-Two Set & Shoot"

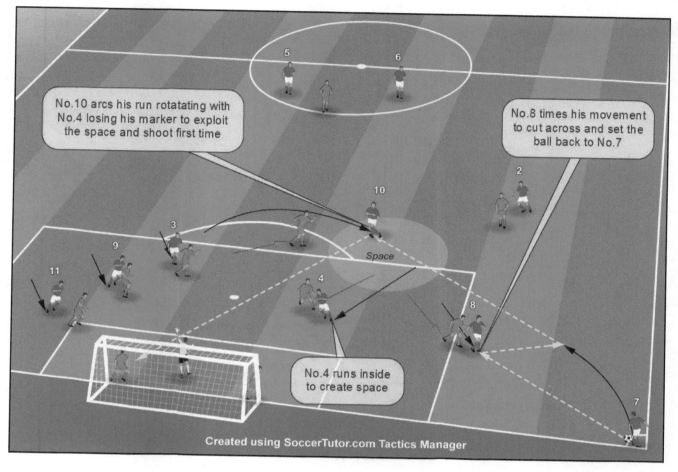

In this short corner scenario up to 4 players perform an important role.

A player (No.8 in the diagram) looks to come short, making a run from near the edge of the box.

- Can the corner taker (7) play a well-weighted pass into No.8's path?

- Can the No.8 then set back a pass to the corner taker in the space? (As shown in the diagram)

- As he does this, can another player positioned nearside on the edge of the box make a decoy run to drag his marker away and open a channel for a pass into the shooter (see No.4 in the diagram).

For this coordinated movement to work well it is important that players' starting positions are well understood. For example, the shooter (10) needs to start as part of the cluster preparing to make decoy runs toward the back post.

As the corner taker (7) receives the return pass from the setter (8), this is the early cue for the shooter (10) to break free and arc his run, making sure to signal where he wants the pass. It is important that he arcs his run as this will ensure he has a good body position to shoot on goal with power. It will also provide him with more awareness of any defenders moving to close him down.

Once No.7 receives the pass back, he weights his pass well for No.10 to run onto and shoot at goal from the edge of the penalty area.

As with the previous short corners, the team should ensure that defensive cover is provided. In this example the full back (No.2) is in an advanced position to draw away another opponent and the 2 centre backs mark the lone red striker.

Short Corner Routine: "One-Two Set & Cross"

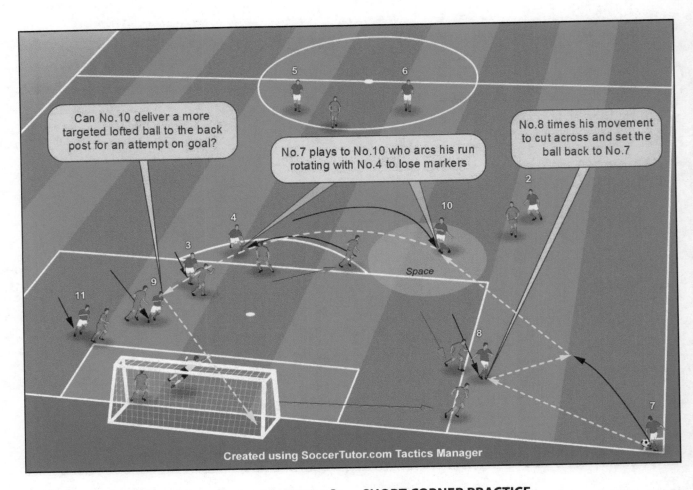

Created using SoccerTutor.com Tactics Manager

Here is a variation of the previous short corner pattern. By setting the ball back into the "arced" run of the No.10, the team also have the option of attacking the back post from a shorter diagonal cross. The advantages here include the element of surprise to confuse defenders, thereby losing markers, and creating space to attack.

The cross is a shorter one from the edge of the box as opposed to from the corner. At youth level especially, this is a more manageable option for a lot of players who perhaps would struggle to deliver longer range crosses. As well as lofting the ball toward the back post, the No.10 might also consider driving the ball along the ground in or around the penalty spot.

Assuming a space opens up there, can a teammate time his run into this area and shoot first time?

All these short corner patterns can be explored using a tactics board to outline the ideas with the players. Use Q&A to reinforce the understanding with your players. The next stage is to nominate the key roles in executing the patterns so everyone is clear what is expected of them.

SHORT CORNER PRACTICE

Set up a corner practice with a realistic number of defenders and attackers and look to explore 2 or 3 options.

At first, defenders should remain "passive" looking to press without tackling or intercepting the ball. As attackers achieve success creating scoring chances, you can progress the practice to a fully competitive one.

Free Kick Routine on the Edge of the Box

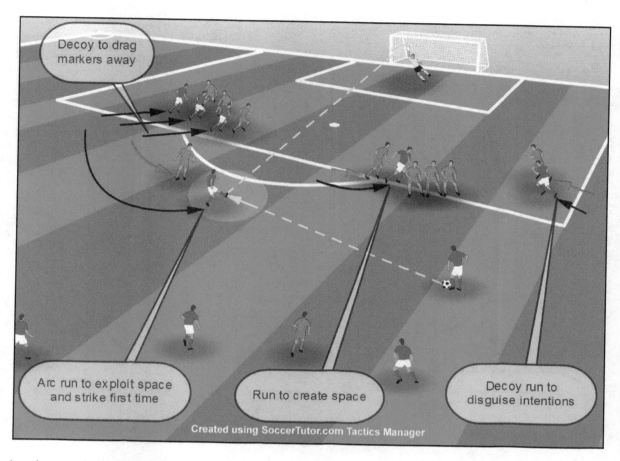

Here is a clever and effective short free-kick routine your players can explore. It can be used when your team get a free kick either side of the 18 yard box. If passing from left to right it is best to have a left footed player as your shooter.

Use a tactics board to set out the routine with your players, covering the following 7 key points:

1. A group of players should be positioned outside the box looking to drive in to finish/head at goal from a cross e.g. toward the back post (see diagram).

2. One designated player positioned at the rear of the group arcs his run into the space available in the centre.

3. Can the free kick taker use "disguise" to look as if he intends to cross a high ball into the box toward the back post and the onrushing group of attackers?

4. Can the group of players look lively as if preparing to attack an aerial pass to the back post? As the free kick taker runs up to take the kick (using disguise as if preparing to cross the ball), can the group start a forward run to drag away opposition markers?

5. At this point, can the free kick taker simply play a weighted ground pass straight across in line with the 18 yard box for the designated shooter to arrive and strike on goal? It is important that the designated player arcs his run sufficiently so he can get a stronger angle to get power into his shot. You can also use an extra wide player (as shown above) to occupy another opponent. This player can make a decoy run inside to commit another marker and help create a further distraction.

6. Can the shooter time his run well and shoot first time if possible? Can he first assess the position of the keeper and then strike with power?

7. Can all other players remain alert for any "secondary chances" in case the keeper or a player blocks the shot and the ball drops for them to finish?

FREE KICK PRACTICE

Try this as a 7 v 7 (+GK) practice setting up the same situation as we have described here. Switch the roles of the teams and see which team can score the most goals from 5 attempts.

Free Kick Routine: "Cross-Over Decoy"

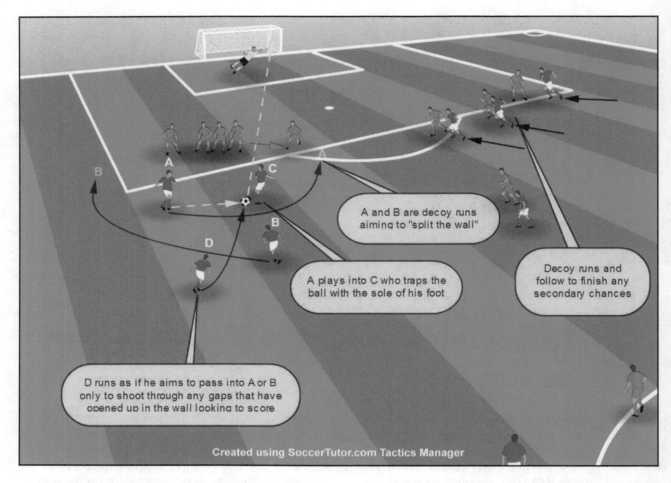

B

A

C

A

B

D

A and B are decoy runs aiming to "split the wall"

A plays into C who traps the ball with the sole of his foot

Decoy runs and follow to finish any secondary chances

D runs as if he aims to pass into A or B only to shoot through any gaps that have opened up in the wall looking to score

Created using SoccerTutor.com Tactics Manager

Here is another free kick routine you might like to explore with your players. Again this involves players making decoy runs, aiming to mislead the opponents trying to defend their goal. The objective here is to split the wall using 2 simultaneous overlapping runs (see diagram). Player D then targets his shot through any promising gap that opens up. Here's how this one works:

- 4 players are positioned around the ball as shown in the diagram.

- Player A takes the free kick with a short pass to player C who traps the ball using the sole of his boot.

- Can player A's pass be the first step of his run so he can quickly overlap the ball making a run towards the penalty area? Simultaneously, can player B sprint across in a diagonally opposite run? Both these runs need to be fast and in front of the striker (Player D).

- Can player D feint as if he intends to run up and lay off a pass into the runs of either player A or player B?

- Chances are these two decoy runs will help split the wall open. Can player D then "go for power" and shoot through the gap against a keeper who is likely to be "unsighted".

- Meanwhile, on the opposite side of the box, 3 players who have occupied their opponent markers have made forward runs driving into the box. Can these 3 players finish off any secondary chances e.g. if the keeper makes a save into their path? Also can players A and B continue their runs in case the ball is parried into their path?

Meanwhile, for security, in case the ball fails to penetrate the wall and the opposition recover possession, the team can count on the following:

1. Players C and D remaining on the edge of the box ready to press and delay any counter attack.

2. The 2 centre backs hold their deep positions to cover any outlet player.

Free Kick Routine: "Mix-Up Disguise"

Created using SoccerTutor.com Tactics Manager

From the edge of the box the instinct is to take a direct shot on goal. However, there are instances in a game where varying the approach could make all the difference. Again, a lot comes down to the kind of team culture you as a coach wish to encourage. The more accustomed your players become to coordinating their movements using good communication, the better they and the team will become. This includes using decoy runs and "disguise" in order to create scoring opportunities.

The following free kick routine may be of interest. It's a cunning little set-up that's simple to explore which allows your players to practice getting around the wall and look to score.

- Players A and B line up together with their backs to goal. They should stand with the ball immediately in front of them, thereby obscuring it from the goalkeeper and the wall.

- Meanwhile player C should line up and prepare himself as if he is intending to run in and strike the ball. The assumption you want to give your opponents is that player A or B will set the ball and

then split out the way to clear a channel for player C to strike the ball on goal. Instead, just as player C breaks into his run-up, player A slips a short sideways pass across player B. Can player B instantly spin and curve a 2 or 3 step run looking to strike the ball around the end of the wall?

For this to work it is important that A and B check the position of the wall as they set up the free kick. Player A needs to be confident he can deliver a well weighted pass for Player B who should practice shooting with power and precision "on the turn". This is a great and mischievous routine to pull off as a team. In a competitive game, the players will enjoy it if it comes off.

For an added element of mischief you can have player A and player B pretend to have a quick argument over what they are planning to do.

- As player C starts his run-up, can Player A pretend to push player B aside in the direction desired and then tap in the sideways pass for player B who quickly goes from position 1 to position 2 and strikes on goal? (See diagram)

VISUAL AWARENESS & GAME INTELLIGENCE

WHAT IS GAME INTELLIGENCE?

In light of what we've covered in this book, I'd like to end with a summary of recent research on visual awareness and game intelligence. I think this research is interesting in the context of what we have been looking at, namely encouraging players toward a more structured and coordinated way of playing. The information I'm about to summarise is rarely, if ever, covered in football coaching books. So here goes, for your more general interest I'll start with some questions:

- What is the difference between an expert and a novice football player?

- What distinguishes a *GENERAL* from a *FOOT SOLDIER* on the pitch?

- We all love watching the top performers, but what distinguishes these players from lesser players?

Research over the past 30 years has identified 5 key areas that define superior game intelligence in football. Here I've put together a summary of these 5 key recent research findings on visual awareness and game intelligence in football. Research indicates that the following perceptual and cognitive skills define high-level elite performance in football (see also Williams, 2000):

1. Elite performers have more success anticipating the actions of their opponents through greater awareness of advance or partial visual cues (see Williams et al., 1999; Savelsbergh et al., 2002, Williams and Burwitz, 1993). For example, skilled players are quicker at reading an opponent's body shape or posture to anticipate the early movements of players off the ball (Abernethy, 1987).

2. Elite performers are quicker and more precise in both the recognition and recall of decisive patterns of play (Williams and Davids, 1995). This ability is considered vital for enhanced anticipation skills in competitive team ball sports such as football.

3. Elite performers are more efficient and effective in their visual search behaviour. Research suggests elite players display more effective "search strategies". Interestingly, these typically involve fewer but longer visual fixations (Williams, 2002; Williams et al., 1999; Abernethy, 2001). By comparison, less skilled players are far more likely to 'ball watch' and show far less alertness to positions and movements of players off the ball (Williams et al., 1994).

4. Elite performers show greater awareness of "situational probabilities". Elite players are more precise in assessing the "probability value" of unfolding patterns of play, another vital cognitive skill underlying anticipation (Williams et al., 2004). For example, in football, this would be the best passing option, or understanding which players are in threatening (e.g goal scoring) and non-threatening positions (e.g. languishing in midfield still digesting their pre-match meal).

5. Elite performers are less susceptible to stress and changes in their emotional state. Research across a number of sporting domains indicates that the "visuo-motor responses" of expert players tend to be more reliable and consistent under pressure (Janelle, 2002). By comparison, novices performing under stressful conditions will tend to increase their saccadic search rate (e.g. their eye movements) and focus on more peripheral, less informative areas on the field of play (Williams & Ward, 2003).

CONCLUSION

RISING TO THE CHALLENGE

This book has covered a fair bit of ground and yet barely touched on the full range of issues and scenarios a player, their team and their coach will likely face. Herein lies the power and the beauty of football - at once it is perfectly simple and yet infinitely variable and complex. In a nutshell, there's always something new to observe, something new to explore, practice and learn through review.

This is what a good coach does working with his players. The over-arching aim should always be to help and encourage their creativity, while also advancing their technical and tactical knowledge. Of course, a coach also has to deal with the specific physical and psychological aspects of the game, which we've not touched on in this book. Neither have we focused on the social aspect that has a huge bearing in football. The vital role played by supportive parents, for example, in assisting the progress of a player, etc. All these areas are very important to better understand the role of a coach. For this reason, it's advisable the coach undertakes their own research and signs up for courses, looking to progress their learning in these areas. There isn't the space here to even begin to do these issues justice. However, there is increasing awareness and resources out there. This should enable coaches to improve their knowledge and effectiveness.

By contrast, this book has narrowed its focus to the purely technical and tactical aspects of the game. There is an argument to say that if the coach gets this aspect right and has good knowledge, he will likely win the respect and enthusiasm of the players. If you can create a lively and positive environment for the players to learn new skills and express their creativity, you will win them over. They will gain in confidence and enthusiasm as they come away from every training session a potentially stronger and more perceptive player. As the coach it is your job to do the best you can to make this aspiration becomes a reality.

So, no pressure, as they say, but also, what a great opportunity and personal challenge to rise to! As a football coach the questions you need to consistently ask yourself are:

- Can I plan and deliver a varied range of practices that address my players needs as well as encourage their creativity?

- Can I keep the sessions lively and maintain good momentum and realism?

- Can I achieve this while at the same time introducing the players to the vital tools (techniques and tactics) they can use to further progress their game?

- When it comes to competitive matches, can I focus on encouraging the players' development and their self-expression?

- Can I ensure to put this above the more basic emotional desire to win?

- Can I enjoy the process of observing and then planning sessions to answer the players' specific needs?

- Can I closely observe areas where I can help improve performance, whether at an individual or overall team level? For example, do I need to encourage players to take on opponents, or, if the back-line is showing a weakness, can I correctly diagnose why?

- And can I then plan or design a specific practice to address these needs and help the players progress and learn so they have more success? Can I do all of this with a positive and constructive attitude at all times, showing the players they are all valued members of the group?

- Can I include all the players every step of the way through discussions and Q&A?

Can I help them see the bigger picture and when they see something I've missed, can I acknowledge, applaud and learn from this myself? Because, as all good coaches appreciate, coaching is a 2 way street and you can learn as much from your players as they can learn from you.

The key to success as a coach is to pre-plan and set out your practices clearly based on the needs of your players. It's vital you let your sessions flow and always encourage creativity and positive energy. So look to break down what you want to cover into simple points that allow the players to learn while having fun. Give them variety and don't keep players standing about for any length of time. Include them all in the practices and make sure the ball is rolling at least 70 - 80 % of the time. The players are looking to you.

- Can you progress their technical and tactical skills while also encouraging their creativity and their love of the game?

- Can you help them learn to better express themselves through playing good, well organised football? Now there's a challenge worth rising to!

Football Coaching Specialists Since 2001

TACTICS MANAGER
Create your own Practices, Tactics & Plan Sessions!

Available for PC and Mac

Work offline
No need for an Internet connection!

Easy to use
Super quick and easy to use!

One-off fee
Yours to keep for life!

5 Day Free Trial
Take a free trial at soccertutor.com!

£59.99 / €75 / $79

Tactics Manager

www.SoccerTutor.com
info@soccertutor.com

Football Coaching Specialists Since 2001

MORE TOP COACHING TITLES

Books Available in Colour Paperback and eBook!

PC | Mac | iPhone | iPad | Android Phone/Tablet | Kobo | Kindle Fire

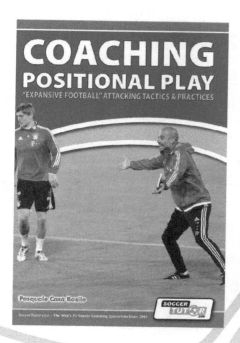

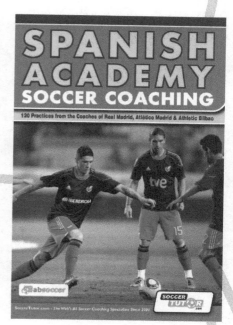

Free Samples
Includes 300+ Free Practices!

DOWNLOAD FREE COACH VIEWER APP
- Search 'Coach Viewer' at your App Store
- For PC download at soccertutor.com

FREE COACH VIEWER APP

www.SoccerTutor.com
info@soccertutor.com

Printed in July 2019
by Rotomail Italia S.p.A., Vignate (MI) - Italy